CALIFORNIA WINE LIST

A Consumer's Guide to

144 Cabernet Sauvignons

CALIFORNIA WINE LIST

A Consumer's Guide to 144 Cabernet Sauvignons

PUBLISHER
John S. Haskell

EDITOR
David Holzgang

CONSULTING EDITOR
Colman Andrews

CONSULTING STATISTICIAN
John Rolph

ADMINISTRATIVE MANAGER
Barbara Dibs

Published by The Cheshire Booksellers, Ltd.
3625 West Sixth Street, Los Angeles, CA 90020
(213) 385-9202

Exclusive Distribution: Wine Appreciation Guild
1377 Ninth Avenue
San Francisco, California 94122
(415) 566-3532

ISBN 0-932664-23-7

INTRODUCTION

This is the fifth edition of CALIFORNIA WINE LIST, a consumer's guide to the wines of California. Our debut issue, which appeared in January 1979, was devoted to Cabernet Sauvignon. Subsequent editions have described and rated Chardonnay, Zinfandel, and assorted jug wines. Now it seems appropriate to return to Cabernet, the undisputed king of California reds, to assess some of the most recent of the many new releases that have appeared since our original consideration of the varietal.

That first Cabernet guide included 114 wines from 81 wineries—or, rather, under 81 labels, since several secondary or private labelings were present—ranging in vintage from 1970 (in one case) through 1976. This volume covers 144 wines under 120 labels, from 1973 (again, in one case) through 1979 (in two cases). Nearly 60 of these labels weren't in the 1980 book; almost half of the top 20 wines in fact, including five of the top seven, are newcomers. On the other hand, some "big names" are missing (as they were from the first Cabernet guide). You won't find Caymus, whose Cabernets are notoriously fine, for instance, nor such highly acclaimed fledglings as Shafer or Matanzas Creek. CALIFORNIA WINE LIST endeavors to be as up-to-date and all-inclusive as possible, but we must function within realistic time limits; if an important winery is not represented here, it's either because that winery had no current regular release or because the vagaries of distribution had temporarily kept it off the shelves of major Southern California retail outlets at the time wines were being collected for our tastings. We don't draw up lists of wines to be included and then go out and get them. Because we are primarily a consumer's guide, we do what the consumer does: We go out and buy whatever we see. If the average wine-buyer can't find a wine, we don't *want* to find it.

The whole idea behind CALIFORNIA WINE LIST, though, is that what the consumer *can* find, when he or she sets out to buy a bottle of California wine of a particular kind, is positively overwhelming. As anyone even remotely interested in California wine surely knows, the state's wine industry continues to grow at an almost alarming rate of speed. There are now 140 wineries in the Napa Valley alone—almost all of them, to put the present volume into perspective, producing Cabernet Sauvignon. Add the wineries of Sonoma, Mendocino, Santa Clara, Monterey, etc., and all the newer areas opening up to quality wine production (San Diego, Santa Barbara, San Luis Obispo, etc.), and you have, well, 144 Cabernets under 120 labels competing for your attention on your wine shop shelves, for instance—when all you're probably looking for is a bottle of good red to go with your lamb chops.

That's where we come in. There is no shortage of published tasting results, wine newsletters, and wine guides available to the consumer. And almost all of them can be of some help in making purchasing decisions. But only CALIFORNIA WINE LIST shows you the large picture, covering this much ground, offering this much scope. We don't just rate 20 or 30 randomly chosen bottles, or loudly praise the half-dozen hot-shot wines of the moment. We try to put wines into context, showing how they compare to their counterparts. More important, we tell you *why* we've rated them as we have. Comparison of wines, we believe, shouldn't be a popularity contest; we don't rate wines with an applause meter, showering prizes on the winners and shunting the losers quietly out the back door. Undeniably there *are* some obvious "winners" and "losers," but the vast majority of the wines we consider, particularly when we're dealing with an important grape variety, are good, sound wines that might appeal slightly more or less to some tasters than others for a variety of reasons. We tell you what those reasons are, so that you can make your own decisions. It's not an accident that our ratings are at the back of the book; they're simply not as important, in our scheme of things.

In any case, as we always point out, we don't claim to be the last word on the subject. Our guiding philosophical principle, which we repeat in every edition of CALIFORNIA WINE LIST, is that "All any tasting really proves is that on a certain date, under certain conditions, a certain group of people liked certain wines better than certain other wines." No comparative tasting can ever be completely objective, much less "accurate." There are statistical adjustments that can be made to obtain something approximating "true" scores in tastings, and the ones we use are explained in the article by statistician John Rolph. But tasting scores, no matter what is done to them, still reflect personal opinions. Because the tasters are wine-business professionals or seasoned amateurs, though, we feel that their opinions— personal, but also educated and experienced—can be of real value to today's wine buyer, whether professional wine-seller, serious amateur, complete beginner, or anything in between. If you drink California wine, in other words, you can profit from CALIFORNIA WINE LIST.

Some general observations: As might be expected with so justly famous a varietal, the overall quality of these 144 Cabernets wasn't bad at all. (To those members of the tasting panel who had participated in the last such event, which dealt with 161 jug wines, this tasting was positively heavenly.) Geographical characteristics stood out rather plainly in some cases— that dusty Napa Valley elegance, those Monterey vegetable smells, etc. Varietal character, on the other hand, often seemed more restrained. There weren't as many big, dark, pungent, sledgehammer-like wines as might have been expected. Whether this was accidental, or was a reflection of the characteristics of recent vintages, or a conscious trend by the winemakers towards softer, more readily drinkable wines is hard to say. But many of the wines, including some of the highest-scoring, tasted more like "wine" than they did like "Cabernet"—a fact which at least some of the tasters viewed with great approval. On the other hand, though many of the wines seemed very well balanced, with nice integration of characteristics, very few showed that intense concentration of flavors that says, This is a great wine! And while it was nice to see that the good old Napa Valley yielded a substantial percentage of the highest scoring wines, it was somehow disconcerting to realize how well the younger wines showed, with 17 of the top 22 wines coming from the 1978 vintage. Is this yet another illustration of the widely-discussed "California palate," which purportedly encourages tasters who drink mostly California wine to prefer tannin and intense young fruit to all other parts of a wine's makeup? Or are the wines of '76 and '77 currently going through an "awkward stage"? Or is it a reflection of some sad truth about the longevity of this supposedly-long-lived California wine? It's impossible to say, but one thing is sure: few if any of the Cabernets tasted seemed completely too young to drink.

EVALUATION

How CALIFORNIA WINE LIST tastings are conducted:

The wines tasted were purchased from reputable Southern California retail wine shops in mid-April of this year. They were tasted in Los Angeles, in groups of between four and seven at a time, arranged according to vintage year and geographical origin, over a two-day period. The tasting panel included two California winemakers, two writers about wine, a former (longtime) wine business executive, and the editor of this publication. The top 21 wines were retasted approximately a week later by a larger panel, including the original tasters (with the editor commenting on the wines but not scoring them) and a selection of 11 wine wholesalers, retailers, consultants, and writers, as well as restaurateurs, sommeliers, and knowledgeable consumers. Tasters were told nothing about the wines they were analyzing, other than the fact that they were California Cabernets, and no taster but the non-scoring editor knew which of the original 144 wines were included in the second tasting.

Each wine was judged in four categories:

1. APPEARANCE: Maximum of 4 points, covering the color of the wine, its depth and clarity and its viscosity.
2. BOUQUET: Maximum of 5 points, covering condition and development of grape aroma and overall bouquet.
3. TASTE: Maximum of 6 points, covering fruit, dryness, body, tannin, acidity and balance.
4. OVERALL QUALITY: Maximum of 5 points, covering finish, finesse, and complexity.

The maximum score is 20 points. Tasting notes follow the sequence of evaluation above.

This system differs from the more usual 20 point system, developed by the University of California at Davis, in that it allows more room for subjective evaluations of overall quality, and thus provides a wider scoring range to distinguish between excellent wines and merely good ones. In any case, we don't believe that the traditional Davis system is appropriate to tastings of this type; it was created for the use of enologists and other scientists in the formal organoleptic evaluation of wine, and doesn't lend itself comfortably to popularly-oriented tastings, which are by their very nature more casual, more subjective, and less concerned with scientifically measurable phenomena. (This doesn't stop many other tasting panels from using the Davis system as formulated but it stops us.)

Users of CALIFORNIA WINE LIST sometimes point out that our scores are always much lower than scores awarded at other similar tastings—rarely topping 15/20 and sometimes sinking to around 6/20 or 7/20, whereas many tasting scores begin around 11/20 and rise to 18/20 or 19/20. This is due partly to the weight given to the aforementioned subjective evaluations (a boring but perfectly well-made wine can easily score in the high 'teens on the Davis scale), and due partly to the fact that members of our tasting panels tend to be pretty tough customers. It is important to remember, though, that a wine rated as "Excellent" with 15/20 by CALIFORNIA WINE LIST is probably every bit as good as one rated "Excellent" and 19/20 by other standards. It should also be noted that a wine has to be extraordinarily good to show well in this much company, and many of the wines that have been rated solidly in the middle range would likely seem extremely good tasted by themselves, or drunk with dinner.

FORMAT

Tasting notes are listed alphabetically by label name, to enable the consumer to use this guide more easily. A second section, beginning on page 53, lists the wines ranked in groups by their total composite score. An additional listing gives the wines ranked by a combination of price per standard 750ml bottle and score, to provide some measure of value. The format of the heading of each entry is as follows:

| LABEL | LABEL | VINTAGE | PRICE | SCORE |
| NAME | DESIGNATION | YEAR | | GROUP |

The Label Designation is included to show any additional label information which may help identify the wine we tasted. Where the wine is non-vintage, the vintage designation is N/V. The price listed is the retail price paid by our shoppers when they bought the wine for tasting in late April, although, since the demise of fair trade regulations for alcoholic beverages in California in July, 1978, prices do vary from city to city and store to store. Six score groups (A to F) were established based on analysis of the composite scores. The first line of description gives both the score group code with a descriptive word and the composite score. Composite scores were derived by the methods listed in the section EVALUATION above; the wines which were selected for retasting have composite scores with two decimal places to aid in distinguishing among wines very close in overall score.

Whenever possible, the listings include estimates of availability from both retail outlets and the winery. The wineries were also queried about production, composition and release data for each wine, and date of next release. When a winery was contacted but did not wish to provide some or all of this data, the listing states that. When we were unable, for whatever reason, to contact the winery, the listing states that the data is unavailable.

STATISTICAL NOTES
by John Rolph, Ph.D.

As remarked in the introduction, "All any tasting really proves is that on a certain date, under certain conditions, a certain group of people liked certain wines better than certain other wines." This reflects not only on the individuality and possible eccentricities of the individual tasters but also on their inevitable inconsistency. That is to say, two different blind tastings of the same wines would, in general, produce significantly different scores, even if the tasters were identical in both cases. With *different* tasters and/or different "lots" of the same wines, even more variation would result.

In reporting the results of CALIFORNIA WINE LIST tastings, certain statistical adjustments are made to minimize the effects of such "taster error." The figures given, then, aren't a simple averaging of the taster's scores; instead, they may be regarded as statistical estimates of the "true score" for each wine—i.e. the relative ranking of each wine against its peers as determined by a given group of tasters. Our purpose here is to give a non-technical description of the kind of adjustments required and the rationale behind them. Recall that all 144 wines were tasted initially by a small group of six tasters. Those wines that scored above 13.2 in the first tasting were later retasted by a larger group of sixteen tasters. There are two aspects of this double tasting format that we must adjust for. First, because the two tasting panels are of different size, the reliability of their average scores differs. This difference must be taken into account when scores from the two tastings are combined and/or compared. Second, only those wines whose scores were high in the first tasting were tasted a second time; through a phenomenon known as the "regression effect," this tasting design results in the twice-tasted wines having, on average, higher scores in the first tasting than in the second.

In understanding the type of statistical adjustments required, an over-simplified model might help (see illustration). First, for a given wine and a given panel of tasters, consider the observed average taster score to be the "true score" plus some factor of "taster variation"; where "taster variation" represents the inevitable changes in scores mentioned above. Assume that the distribution of true scores follows a symmetric curve. Under this model, the distribution of observed scores, (i.e. those given to the wine by the tasters) will tend to be more spread out than the distribution of the true scores. The fewer the tasters, and hence the larger the taster variation (in general), the more the distribution of average taster score is spread out.

The illustration presents a hypothetical example of such a situation. Two distributions of observed scores are depicted for tasting panels of two sizes. Note that the curve labeled "large number of tasters" is not as spread out as that labeled "small number of tasters." If the two panels taste the same group of wines, and you line up both sets of scores together, the smaller panel would have given both the highest and the lowest scores. But, since the wines tasted by both panels did not differ in true score on the average, the smaller panel having the extreme scores is an accident that can only be explained by the inevitably larger taster variation of this panel. The results of this accidental variation can be eliminated if each of the observed scores is "shrunk" towards the overall average (in our example, vi

10 points) in such a way that the rescaled scores for each of the panels look like the true score distribution. With such an adjustment, the rescaled scores of the panels are comparable—and the problems caused by the different sizes of the tasting panels are eliminated.

To understand the adjustments made to alleviate the second problem, that of the regression effect, suppose that the average taster variation in the initial (smaller) tasting is just as likely to be positive as negative, and tends to be about half a point (.5) in size. Thus, if a wine has a true score of 10.5, it is just as likely to have an observed score of 10 as 11. Similarly, a wine that has a true score of 11.5 is just as likely to score 11 as 12.

Take all the wines that scored 11 on the first tasting, for instance. The two possible explanations of this score are: (a.) the true score was below 11, with a positive taster variation; or (b.) the true score was above 11, with negative taster variation. As the illustration indicates, many more wines have scores of 10.5 than 11.5, so the first explanation is, on balance, the more likely to be correct. This reasoning can be made precise and leads to the conclusion that if the observed score is above average on the first tasting, a second tasting will yield a score that is, on the average, lower than the score on the first tasting. Or, to put it another way, the first score in this situation will tend to overestimate the true score, so it should be adjusted downward.

A technical description of how the observed scores are statistically adjusted is available on request from the publisher of CALIFORNIA WINE LIST.

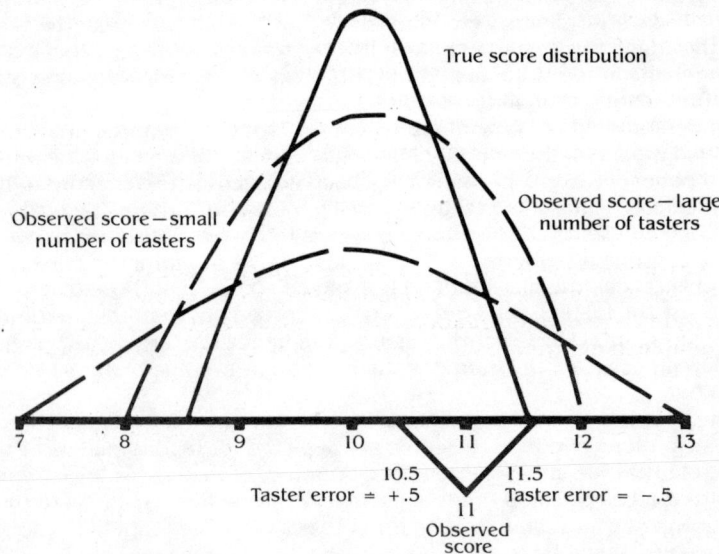

Alatera   1978 $10.00   D

Score group D: Good   Composite score 11.4

Deep purple; very clear with medium legs.
Peculiar aroma; smells of varnish and vegetables.
Medium body with some good fruit; some varietal flavor. Moderate tannin
but a strong oak or wood flavor. A hollowness in the middle leaves the
impression that the flavors are only uneasily put together.
Moderate finish with a woody character in the aftertaste. This is a clean,
standard Cabernet, flawed by an unpleasant nose and otherwise unexciting.

**Winery data not available. Label indicates production of 2832 bottles
(236 cases) with a Napa regional appellation.**

Almaden   1978   Monterey $4.09   B

Score group B: Superior   Composite score 13.48

Good hue, marvelous garnet or ripe plum color; slightly pink around the
edges. Heavy legs but lacks brilliance; perhaps could use better filtration
or racking.
Deep, fruity, quite a lot going on; a hint of cassis and cedar in the nose.
Ample, with lots of wood; some cigar box Cabernet aromas. Monterey
nose; vegetal, minty, oaky, a slight weedy character. Pleasant impact;
slow to open but extremely complex.
Medium body and a well-structured wine with fair fruit. Slight central
coast character; pleasant fruit and wood. Complex with some good
flavors but an overriding vegetal taste; light, airy; not a big presence in
the mouth. More drinkable but perhaps not as exciting as some of the
other wines; lacks tannin and depth.
Nice finish but not quite integrated; well made; well balanced; will be
extremely elegant and fragrant in a few years. Light to medium good
flavor with an aftertaste of Monterey county grasses. Big, dark, fat
attractive wine; rather soft and ready, rich texture though not
intense Cabernet.

**Winery produced 20,000 cases which were bottled in Spring 1980 and
released in Summer 1980. Composition is 100% Cabernet with a
Monterey regional appellation. The wine is a current release and is
available in distribution and at many retail outlets. No date was given
for the next release.**

Alexander Valley   1978 $6.49   C

Score group C: Very Good   Composite score 12.2

Deep purple; very clear with heavy legs.
Good nose with some weediness in the aroma but not much of Cabernet.
Has a damp cellar smell, nice and cool and inviting but a bit moldy in
the corners.
Medium body with good berry-like fruitiness. Interesting flavor suggests
but does not state the variety.
Moderate finish; earthy, rather pleasant aftertaste.

Winery produced 3300 cases which were bottled in August 1980 and

released in November 1980. Composition is 90% Cabernet and 10% Merlot; the regional appellation is Alexander Valley. The wine is a current release and is available both in distribution and at the winery. The next release is scheduled for November 1981.

Beaulieu Vineyard   1975   Private Reserve $15.00   C

Score group C: Very Good   Composite score 12.5

Medium to royal purple; very clear with medium to heavy legs.
Subdued nose, with a light Cabernet aroma. A touch of honeyed fruit and minty flowers in the back.
Moderate to thin body; a lot of wood and tannin in the mouth. Light fruit and high acid detract from an otherwise nice combination of flavors. Perhaps a little too much wood.
Sharp, medium finish with a tannic aftertaste. A solid, if unspectacular, wine with some good Cabernet flavor.

Winery does not wish to give amount of production; the wine was bottled in August 1979. Composition is 100% Cabernet from estate vineyards at Rutherford, in the Napa Valley. This is the current release of the Private Reserve, and is available in very limited quantities at most fine wine stores. The next release is the 1976 vintage Private Reserve and is scheduled for early Fall 1981.

Beaulieu Vineyard   1977   Estate Bottled $7.00   C

Score group C: Very Good   Composite score 11.9

Medium purple with a touch of ruby; very clear with medium legs.
Light nose with some nice black cherry aroma and a touch of earthiness.
Thin to moderate body; nice fruit but light flavor. Nicely sharp on the palate with adequate tannin. Seems a bit over-processed.
Moderate finish with a pleasant lemon and wood aftertaste. Fresh, clean wine with a generally Cabernet quality but too small.

Winery does not wish to give the amount of production; the wine was bottled in January 1980. Composition is 100% Cabernet from the Rutherford area of the Napa Valley. This is a current release and is in general distribution and is available at the winery. The next release will be the 1978 vintage and is scheduled for early Fall 1981.

Beringer   1977   Napa $6.49   D

Score group D: Good   Composite score 10.3

Medium ruby with an orange-brown edge; very clear with medium to thin legs.
Nose is rough and light in fruit; beginning to oxidize and shows lots of bottle bouquet but little complexity or charm.
Medium body and some fruit; tannic. Has some elegance and nice balance but is light and lacks flavor; tastes old, like a wine aged past its prime.
Medium finish, rather rough. An average, blended and rather old Cabernet.

Winery produced over 10,000 cases which were bottled in mid-1979 and released in December 1979. Composition is 100% Cabernet with a Napa regional appellation. This is not the current release and the wine is no

longer available in distribution. The current releases are the 1977
Reserve and the 1977 Estate Bottled Cabernets.

Boeger   1978 $7.49   D
Score group D: Good   Composite score 11.6

Medium to deep purple; very clear with medium to heavy legs.
Light, rather closed nose with some fruit. A briary and woody quality
predominates.
Medium body with good balance. Some nice fruit, perhaps a bit light, with
a strong stemmy flavor and a taste of wood.
Moderate finish; rough, stemmy aftertaste. Pleasant enough, but the
wood and stems overpower any varietal qualities.

Winery produced 966 cases which were bottled in September 1980 and
released in January 1981. Composition is 93% Cabernet and 7% Merlot
with a regional appellation of El Dorado County. The wine is a current
release and is available both in distribution and at the winery. The next
release is scheduled for Winter 1981.

David Bruce   1977   San Luis Obispo $7.50   F
Score group F: Poor   Composite score 7.2

Very deep purple; clear with heavy legs.
Strong and unpleasant smell; a brown mustard and tobacco aroma with
a vinegary overtone indicative of excessive volatile acidity.
High volatile acidity almost overpowers a sharp, unpleasant ethyl acetate
flavor. No fruit and extreme woodiness make an unpleasant impression.
Overall, judged to be unacceptably unpleasant.

Winery produced 1200 cases which were released in April 1981.
Composition is 100% Cabernet with a regional appellation of San Luis
Obispo. The wine is not the most current release although it is available
both in distribution and at the winery. The current release is the 1978
vintage with the same appellation. The next release is scheduled for
Fall 1981.

David Bruce   1978   Santa Cruz $11.95   D
Score group D: Good   Composite score 11.5

Deep to medium purple, with much lighter highlights; very clear with
medium legs.
Raspberries and strawberries in the aroma with a lot of wood and a smell
of hazelnuts in the nose. Some complexity developing.
Medium body with nice fruit and flavor but very high tannin and an oaky
flavor that overpowers everything else.
Medium finish with a woody, hazelnut aftertaste. A pleasant, common
Cabernet.

Winery produced 350 cases which were bottled in November 1980 and
released in April 1981. Composition is 100% Cabernet with a regional
appellation of Santa Cruz County. The wine is a current release and is
available both in distribution and at the winery. The next release is
scheduled for Fall 1981.

Burgess   1978   Napa $9.00   C

Score group C: Very Good   Composite score 12.3

Deep ruby with purple highlights; very clear with heavy legs.
Clean but simple nose with strong vegetal, peppery smells.
Moderate body; solid, well-balanced, showing some wood. Fruit is either
lacking or closed up and flavor lacks highlights
Good finish, rather short, with a stemmy aftertaste. A good standard
Cabernet.

Winery produced 4500 cases which were bottled in July 1980 and
released in February 1981. Composition is 86% Cabernet and 14%
Merlot with a regional appellation of Napa. The wine is a current release
and is available both in distribution and at the winery. The next release
is scheduled for February 1982.

Cakebread Cellars   1978 $12.00   A

Score group A: Excellent   Composite score 15.47

Lovely color, great depth; really nice brick and blue; brilliant with
heavy legs.
Nice, fruity nose, cherry-like character; very attractive with lots of wood
and a weedy Cabernet aroma, though somewhat subdued. Excellent fruit,
berry and eucalyptus; earthy. Sparse but genuine bouquet; velvet, violets
and oak. Another "closed in" nose but you know it won't stay
down forever.
Big wine; will probably develop nicely; complex and good weave of
flavors. Fruit is hard and unforgiving; good flavors of cedar and tannin
but not much Cabernet. Withheld at the moment, but in excellent
balance if the hints of fruit are real. Very tannic; light in acid but creamy.
A nice, stemmy, big wine but needs some age; too young now but should
be great in time.
Finish is a little short, and Cabernet character is lost in the finish as the
wood overpowers wine; otherwise damned nice wine. Good promise for
future development; should be very good. Not very complex, through no
fault of its own, and lacks finesse but finesse is not the point right now.
An overpowering wine but could really develop.

Winery produced 800 cases which were bottled in June 1980 and
released in October 1980. Composition is 100% Cabernet with a Napa
regional appellation. The wine is the most recent release and is
available in distribution. The next release will be the 1979 vintage and
is scheduled for August 1981.

Cakebread Cellars   1978   JT-L1 $12.00   B

Score group B: Superior   Composite score 14.86

Good dark blue-red; very deep and full with tinges of purple; nice color,
nearly perfect. Heavy legs and good clarity.
Nice fruity/oaky nose; forward, charming; some tar-like richness hides
behind lots of spicy oak (several tasters suggested new French oak).
Outstanding nose; minty and eucalyptus; beautiful with excellent fruit.

Clean; not much complexity but more age will develop. Stalky,
young—this will pass.
Medium to full body; rich, rather chocolatey flavor. Some obvious
substance but very tannic; intense fruit with oak overtones. Good acid;
good structure; wonderful flavor and wood, but tannic. May age out,
much soft grape tannin. Almost seems to have a touch of sweetness;
tannin and acid are very high; fruit is very closed in. Interesting flavors
and textures.
Long, lingering finish. Slight candy-like sweetness in finish. Big, but
relatively soft with potential. Complex and interesting; nice finish. Very
drinkable and substantial wine. Its qualities are all good, but they need to
be intensified.

**Winery produced 2200 cases which were bottled in June 1980 and
released in October 1980. Composition is 100% Cabernet with a Napa
regional appellation. The label designation shown above, JT-L1,
distinguishes this release from the wine in the preceding listing. The
wine is the most recent release and is available in distribution. The next
release will be the 1979 vintage and is scheduled for August 1981.**

Callaway	**1978**	**Estate Bottled**	**$7.49**	**D**

Score group D: Good   Composite score 11.7

Medium to deep purple; very clear with heavy legs.
Very heavy, almost chocolate aroma; smells overripe and oxidized.
Medium to full body with a rich, woody flavor. Surprisingly soft, with
a good balance of tannin and fruit. Doesn't quite deliver the punch implied
by the nose. One reviewer commented, "A sheep in wolf's clothing."
Medium to long finish; rich but tannic aftertaste. Overall, a big but
ungracious wine with a touch of raisins in the flavor; neither typical of
the variety nor even obviously Cabernet.

**Winery produced 2500 cases which were bottled in January 1981 and
released in March 1981. Composition is 100% Cabernet; the wine is
estate bottled with a regional appellation of Temecula. The wine is
a current release and is available both in distribution and at the winery.
The next release is scheduled for April 1982.**

J Carey Cellars	**1978**	**Alamo Pintado Vineyards**	**$6.00**	**C**

Score group C: Very Good   Composite score 13.0

Deep purple; brilliant with heavy legs.
Sharp, rather unpleasant nose; rough with a touch of tea and sulphur.
Some fruit showing with a herbaceous aroma.
Medium body; good, rich fruit and a good Cabernet flavor backed with
a minty, rather herbal quality. Well integrated, with good acidity and
some wood.
Long finish; an unpleasant and rather musty taste overtakes the fine fruit
at the end. Wine is just emerging; big and dark, it has some real
potential. Not an exciting wine at this point, but a good standard.

**Winery produced 450 cases which were bottled in January 1980 and
released in August 1980. Composition is 100% Cabernet; the wine is**

estate bottled with a regional appellation of the Santa Ynez Valley. This is not the current release and is no longer available either at the winery or in distribution. The next release is scheduled for April 1982.

Carneros Creek   **1978**   **Turnbull / Fay Vineyards**   **$8.50**   **C**

Score group C: Very Good   Composite score 12.3

Deep purple; very clear with heavy legs.
Closed, rather perfumey nose with some complexity. Unusual fruit but not an unpleasant aroma.
Medium body with a touch of fruit and a stemmy flavor. Quite tannic and not very charming but a big mouthful of wine.
Moderate finish with a heavy, almost dirty aftertaste and excessive tannin returning behind.

The wine was bottled in June 1980 and 2500 cases were released in July 1980. Composition is 85% Cabernet and 15% Merlot with a regional appellation of Napa from the named vineyards. The wine is a current release but is no longer available in distribution or at the winery. An additional allocation of this wine will be released in 1982; the next scheduled release is the 1979 Cabernet in July 1981.

Cassayre-Forni   **1978**   **$9.00**   **A**

Score group A: Excellent   Composite score 15.68

Good dark shoulders and a black depth; a beautiful, rich, deep color. Nice substance; real "purple" in the legs; brilliant with heavy legs.
Apples and spice (allspice or cardamom) mixed with hints of violet and oak in a varietal nose. Fragrant and herbaceous; a very typical, very youthful, solid benchmark Cabernet with lots of vanilla / wood in the nose. Sweet impact with evolution of various flowers, even roses, into the decidedly Cabernet nose. Very elegant; light, delicate fruit and wood; slightly subdued.
Nice rich, good flavor and balance; high tannin. Good body and some good underlying fruit but pretty hidden right now; mostly you can taste the vanilla from the oak. Complex flavors; short on the middle of the palate. Well put together; good balance; almost flawless in its simplicity. Big, dry, tannic with fine balance. Delivers to the palate what was promised on the nose; still young but well made.
Long finish, dominated by a touch of fruit and high tannin. A lovely wine with a fine, even future ahead. Nice to the finish; a dinner wine with sound balance: grape tannins vs. wood; shows considerable promise. Very dark; fruit and flavor lie hid in night. A charming wine; as one taster put it, "Could be a nice one—it's got a beat you can dance to."

Winery produced 1150 cases which were bottled in June 1980 and released in September 1980. Composition is 100% Cabernet and the wine is 100% from the Napa Valley. The wine is a current release but is no longer available in distribution, although limited amounts may be available at retail. The next release is scheduled for September 1981.

Chappellet — 1977 — $11.95 — C

Score group C: Very Good — Composite score 11.9

Deep purple; clear with heavy legs.
Soft, moderate nose with a deep, dark grapiness. A bit of green olive and wood in the shadows; interesting but not strongly varietal.
Good body; very tannic. Fruit hardly discernable due to the tannin; what is there seems a combination of oranges and apples.
Long finish; extremely tannic at the end with no fruit to sustain it. Very heavy, very stiff wine which seems to lack fruit and varietal flavor—or it's all lost in the tannin.

Winery produced 4500 cases which were bottled in July 1979 and released in August 1980. Composition is 100% Cabernet with a regional appellation of Napa. The wine is not the current release but is available both in distribution and at the winery. The current release is the 1978 vintage, released in April 1981.

Chateau Chevalier — 1978 — $12.50 — C

Score group C: Very Good — Composite score 12.8

Full, rather rich, royal purple; brilliant with heavy legs.
Shy nose with overtones like a sandalwood or cedar chest. Dry and spicy. The varietal aroma is present, but not very forthcoming.
Medium to light body with just a bit of spritz. Tannic with a bit of fruit but a bell pepper taste; very spicy and active in the mouth; still sharply youthful.
Moderate, tannic finish with a sandalwood aftertaste. Not a lot of varietal quality, but a very attractive red wine.

Winery produced 2808 cases which were bottled in September 1979 and released in September 1980. Composition is 100% Cabernet with a regional appellation of Napa. The wine is a current release but is sold out both in distribution and at the winery. The next release is scheduled for Fall 1981.

Chateau Montelena — 1976 — $10.00 — C

Score group C: Very Good — Composite score 13.0

Deep purple with a touch of ruby in the highlights; very clear with moderate to heavy legs.
Stingy bouquet with a light but definite Cabernet aroma; closed but shows some depth of character and a touch of vegetables (leeks) behind. No off odors, but a bit nondescript.
Medium body with a nice flavor and satisfactory Cabernet character, but light in fruit. Moderate tannin and some wood with good acid in balance.
Sharp, rather stemmy aftertaste with some wood in a lingering finish.
Biggish wine but backwards; more promise than performance—maybe with age nice things will happen.

Winery produced 4600 cases which were bottled in June 1979 and released in August 1980. Composition is 100% Cabernet with a North Coast regional appellation. This is not the current release and is sold out in distribution, although it is still available at the winery and is still available in limited amounts at retail. The current release is the 1977 Sonoma Cabernet, and a 1977 Napa Cabernet is scheduled for release in August 1981.

Chateau St. Jean   1977   Glen Ellen Vineyards $13.50   C

Score group C: Very Good   Composite score 12.0

Medium purple with ruby highlights; very clear with heavy legs.
Light nose with some attractive elements—some fruitiness, some stalkiness. Definite but not very full varietal nose with a touch of eucalyptus. Moderate body, light and lively flavor. Stemmy and tannic with lots of wood; not a lot of fruit, but what is there is attractive and varietal.
Long to medium finish; some wood and a smoky quality in the aftertaste. Could be nice if it develops somewhat.

Winery produced 415 cases which were bottled in April 1979 and released in Spring 1980. Composition is 100% Cabernet with a regional appellation of Sonoma from the named vineyards. This is a current release, but is no longer available in distribution or at the winery. Some small amounts may be available at retail. No further release of Cabernet is scheduled at this time, and we were informed that the winery is cutting back its production of red wines.

Chateau St. Jean   1977   Jack London Vineyards $9.50   C

Score group C: Very Good   Composite score 12.7

Medium to full ruby; very clear with medium legs.
Rough, rather high alcohol nose with some definite Cabernet aroma showing. Pine and ocean spray in the background.
Medium body; nice, full flavors of pine and earth and an apple-like astringency. Very acidic and very tannic.
Moderate finish, perhaps a bit short; some nice varietal fruit in the aftertaste. Good fruit but rough in the mouth and not yet pulled together. Probably better in a year or two if the fruit outlasts the wood.

Winery produced 654 cases which were bottled in July of 1979 and released in the Spring of 1980. Composition is 100% Cabernet with a regional appellation of Sonoma from the named vineyards. This is a current release, but is no longer available in distribution or at the winery. Some small amounts may be available at retail. No further release of Cabernet is scheduled at this time, and we were informed that the winery is cutting back its production of red wines.

Christian Brothers   1975 $7.35   F

Score group F: Poor   Composite score 8.9

Medium ruby with orange highlights; very clear with thin legs.
Soapy nose with a cigar box quality; might be some nice complexity developing but almost totally obscured by off odors of cheese and burnt wood.
Thin and light in fruit; good balance but lacks varietal flavor, and has an odd, unpleasant quality like a slightly burnt caramel custard.
Thin, tannic finish. Overall, this would be an average wine if there were

not something unpleasant in the background.

Winery produced 9400 cases which were bottled in January 1980 and released in November 1980. Composition is 70% Cabernet Sauvignon, 21.3% Cabernet Franc and 8.7% Merlot. The wine is a current release and is available both in distribution and at the winery. A schedule for the next release was not given.

Cilurzo-Piconi	1978	First Crush	$6.50	D

Score group D: Good   Composite score 10.9

Medium to deep ruby; very clear with medium legs.
Moderate varietal fruit in nose, with a briary, woody overtone. Leaves a rather unpleasant, dirty or tanky impression.
Light in the mouth and light in flavor; sharp and fleeting with some volatile acidity showing. Flavor is not bad, but murky and ill-defined rather than crisp.
Moderate to long finish with an herbal aftertaste.

Winery produced 500 cases which were bottled in December 1979 and released in January 1980. Composition is 100% Cabernet with a regional appellation of Temecula. This is a current release but is no longer available in distribution or at the winery. With the next release, a 1979 Cabernet from the La Cresta Vineyards, scheduled for Fall 1981, the winery name and label will change to Cilurzo Vineyard and Winery.

Clos Du Bois	1977	Proprietor's Reserve	$18.00	D

Score group D: Good   Composite score 10.8

Light purple with a touch of ruby; very clear with medium legs.
Light, slightly raisiny nose with an older quality and overtones like fresh, crusty bread—but not yeasty.
Light fruit with a hint of peach flavor; thin in body. A very light, fleeting quality; almost seems to evaporate in the mouth.
Light finish of minimal interest. Too thin for Cabernet, and too short on flavor to be of much interest.

Winery does not wish to provide production data; the wine was bottled in November 1980 and released in January 1981. Composition is 100% Cabernet with a Sonoma regional appellation. The wine is a current release and is available both in distribution and at the winery. The next release is scheduled for Fall 1981.

Clos Du Bois	1978	Alexander Valley	$7.50	C

Score group C: Very Good   Composite score 11.8

Medium purple with royal purple highlights; very clear with medium to heavy legs.
Light, simple nose with definite Cabernet aroma; overtones of cherries or meadow grass.
Medium body with decent flavor and tannin. Good balance but very light in the mouth without any backbone or stuffing, and not much varietal character.

Moderate finish with an earthy aftertaste. Clean, fresh, honest wine without intensity or complexity.

Winery does not wish to provide production data; the wine was bottled in December 1980 and released in January 1981. Composition is 75% Cabernet and 25% Merlot with an Alexander Valley regional appellation. The wine is a current release and is available both in distribution and at the winery. The next release is scheduled for Fall 1981.

Clos Du Val	1977	Reserve	$20.00	B

Score group B: Superior   Composite score 13.22

Deep color; black edge into a deep purple with royal highlights; very clear with heavy legs.
Good woody/spicy aromas, plus pleasant Cabernet character too; a little like green olives. Some fruit; some wood (hints of cedar) in nose; non-assertive. Excellent Cabernet and wood; bit of bouquet—have to dig for it though, very delicate violets coming through.
Full body; very dry and dusty with a tannic quality; some nice fruit and a good earthy flavor. Flavor follows nose beautifully. Seems a bit awkward at the moment, and only fair balance. Dry, ingratiating; some carry-over of mustiness in flavor; good varietal berries coming through.
Clean finish; some hints of interest: finishes well in mouth. One vision of a good Cabernet: heaps of fruit; some wood; interesting character. A solid spicy Cabernet of some distinction. Its strength is cleanliness and balance.

Winery does not wish to provide production data; the wine was bottled in January 1980 and released in September 1980. Composition is 85% Cabernet and 15% Merlot. The wine is not a current release but is available both in distribution and at the winery. Schedule for the next release is not yet available.

Clos Du Val	1978	$12.00	B

Score group B: Superior   Composite score 14.68

Royal purple and ruby; clear color. Bright, classic but youthful; modest viscosity.
Unique nose with a chocolate-minty, closed up character; some quality is evident—just a hint of wood and a dash of spice. Busy; lots going on but none of it terribly attractive. Not a typical nose, perhaps from the wood or Michael Robbin's term "ecological imbalance." Closed in totally—can't smell it: shows some fruit, cloves, and some oak.
A nice flavor; rather rich but very tannic with hints of nice fruit working in there. Strong acid backbone; only a medium bodied wine but it seems much larger. Dusty with some black cherry fruit and a "seedy" tannic component. Clean, light, drinkable; tastes much younger than color and bouquet would lead you to expect. Perhaps a bit too tannic for its size, but well made and rather pleasant with nice balance except for tannin. Sharp aftertaste in a long finish with some complexity; has a harmony of all its elements. A well put together wine; clean and simple. Good finish but light; drinking well at this time. A well-made wine in a drinkable style. Could be a very popular and well-accepted wine.

Winery produced 12,000 cases which were bottled in August 1980 and released early in 1981. Composition is approximately 87% Cabernet and 13% Merlot with a Napa regional appellation. The wine is a current release and is available both in distribution and at the winery. The schedule for the next release is not available.

Concannon   1973   Limited Bottling $9.99   E

Score group E: Fair   Composite score 9.9

Medium ruby with orange edges; clear with medium legs.
Clean vinous aroma, with a touch of herbal or evergreen behind. Simple but pleasant.
Light and thin and lacking in flavor. Soft, well balanced with a touch of fruit but nothing even vaguely varietal.
Thin finish; a vaguely dirty aftertaste like wet concrete. Common, mediocre and not varietal.

Winery produced 3723 cases which were bottled in July 1978 and released in Fall 1979. Composition is 100% Cabernet; the wine is estate bottled with a California appellation. The wine is a current release and is available both in distribution and at the winery. The next release is scheduled for late in 1981.

Conn Creek   1977 $12.00   D

Score group D: Good   Composite score 11.6

Royal purple with some deeper highlights; very clear with medium legs.
Moldy or earthy smell with some definite Cabernet aroma behind.
Medium body; rather astringent with substantial tannin and acid. Flavor is dominated by a moldy, woody quality that finishes with a bitter flavor like endive.
Short finish with the bitterness mellowing to smoke and wood in the aftertaste. Not a bad wine, but overpowered by the woody/moldy quality.

Winery produced 2900 cases which were bottled in April 1980 and released in October 1980. Composition is 100% Cabernet with a Napa regional appellation. The wine is a current release and is available both in distribution and at the winery. The next release is scheduled for September 1981.

Cuvaison   1976 $9.00   D

Score group D: Good   Composite score 11.4

Medium purple with a touch of orange; clear but a bit of a haze, medium legs.
Vinous aroma with a hot, dusty quality; no individual grape smell, but the beginning of a nicely integrated, although not complex, bouquet.
Medium body, reasonably big but lacks sufficient acid to carry the wood and fruit. Tannic, with a spicy, slightly minty taste.
Medium finish with a sharp, harsh aftertaste like Angostura bitters. A fair wine without real varietal character.

Winery produced 7000 cases which were bottled in July 1978 and released in November 1980. Composition is 85% Cabernet and 15%

Merlot with a Napa regional appellation. The wine is a current release and is available both in distribution and at the winery. The next release is scheduled for November 1981.

Cygnet Cellars 1977 $5.50 E

Score group E: Fair Composite score 9.3

Deep ruby; brilliant with medium legs.
Full, rather spicy nose with a strong vegetable aroma, suggestive of grapes from the Monterey region.
Medium body, but thin in flavor and with a bit of harshness. Has a strong vegetable flavor carrying over from the nose; no varietal components.
Short finish with a touch of eucalyptus in the aftertaste. Overall, dull · and insipid.

Winery produced 300 cases which were bottled in Fall 1978 and released in Spring 1979. Composition is 100% Cabernet with a Central Coast regional appellation. The wine is a current release and is available both in distribution and at the winery. The next release is not scheduled at this time.

Davis Bynum 1978 $7.75 C

Score group C: Very Good Composite score 12.1

Medium purple with lighter ruby highlights; very clear with medium legs.
Moderate nose with a good varietal quality; rough, rather vegetal or burnt overtones.
Medium body with some good fruit; dull and a bit harsh.
Moderate to short finish, with a nice, lightly stalky aftertaste. Basically sound but dull wine.

Winery data not available. Label indicates a Sonoma regional appellation.

Dehlinger Winery 1978 $8.00 C

Score group C: Very Good Composite score 12.8

Deep purple; brilliant with heavy legs.
Lightly fruity nose with hints of cherries and herbs; oaky, rather dusty character and not a lot of varietal aroma.
Clean, medium body; rather light and thin with a very woody or herbal flavor. Very high wood with substantial tannin. Some light, cherry-like flavors, but overall the wood overpowers the fruit.
Astringent and woody finish. A basically sound wine but lacks fruit for the long run.

Winery produced 2000 cases which were bottled in July 1980 and released in November 1980. Composition is 100% Cabernet with a Sonoma regional appellation. The wine is a current release and is available in limited quantities in distribution. The next release is scheduled for November 1981.

Diamond Creek   1978   **Red Rock Terrace**   **$12.00**   **C**

Score group C: Very Good   Composite score 12.0

Deep purple with slightly lighter amethyst highlights; very clear with
heavy legs.
Cinnamon and cedar in the nose with a nice, briary, black cherry varietal
aroma. Some slightly spoiled or off smells in the background.
Medium body; nice fruit and flavor but high in wood. Flavor is hanging
back behind the wood.
Moderate finish with wood and spice aftertaste and a touch of vanilla
lingering on the palate. Overall impression is of a rather retarded
development, and perhaps not all in balance when it evens out.

Winery data not available.

Dry Creek   1977   **Vintner's Selection**   **$10.00**   **D**

Score group D: Good   Composite score 10.7

Light to medium ruby; very clear with medium legs.
Strong nose with an aroma of vegetables and some chemical overtones;
perhaps a hint of fruit in the background.
Medium body, medium tannin; has some substance but only light fruit.
Not much varietal character.
Medium finish with a dry, tannic aftertaste. Overall a good red wine but
harsh and lacking varietal quality.

**Winery produced approximately 1700 cases which were bottled in
August 1979 and released in September 1980. Composition is 100%
Cabernet with a Sonoma regional appellation. The wine is a current
release and is available both in distribution and at the winery. The next
release is tentatively scheduled for 1983.**

Dry Creek   1978   **$7.25**   **D**

Score group D: Good   Composite score 11.2

Deep ruby with purple highlights; very clear with medium legs.
A light varietal aroma with a musty overtone; some nice fruit but slightly
seedy.
Medium body and good balance but lacks some fruit; low in acid and
a bit tame.
Moderate finish but stiff and charmless and lacking in varietal qualities.

**Winery produced 9300 cases which were bottled in July 1980 and
released in January 1981. Composition is 89% Cabernet and 11%
Merlot with a Sonoma regional appellation. The wine is a current release
and is available both in distribution and at the winery. The next release
is scheduled for Fall 1981.**

Duckhorn Vineyards   1978   **$10.50**   **A**

Score group A: Excellent   Composite score 15.41

Young and dark—deep, clear garnet; a nice color that looks perfect.
Substantial, looks like a big wine; brilliant with heavy legs.

Wood and vines and herbs; the varietal quality is behind, but still a good nose; seductive; lightly spicy; violets and tea. Reserved, but with an impending complexity and a bit of a woody, floral, slightly weedy character with overtones of cloves in the aroma. Provocative—berry and grass and only a slight indication of oak; an elusive bouquet worth waiting for.

Good, solid wine with a medium to light body; some cherry-like fruit and high in tannin. Good acid, and plenty of fruit; in balance but light in wood. Dry, tannic, enough fruit for the acid; very complete in all taste categories; rich. A very big wine that shows considerable promise. One taster remarked, "Many would find the aftertaste too overpowering; (but) I would like more oak."

Rich, good berry-like, powerful fruit in a medium long finish and with a spice aftertaste. Attractive rather than interesting; subdued but has finesse; solid and well-balanced without "bumps." Has a good feel, but not much depth yet; youthful. One taster enthused, "Plummy indeed! a bumper tosser for the gods."

Winery produced 800 cases which were bottled in April 1980 and released in March 1981. Composition is 100% Cabernet with a Napa regional appellation. The wine is a current release but is no longer available in distribution; it is still available at the winery on a limited basis. The next release will be a 1979 Merlot, which is scheduled for September 1981.

| **Durney** | **1978** | **Carmel Valley** | **$11.95** | **A** |

Score group A: Excellent   Composite score 15.37

Very deep, very clear, very young magenta; medium in depth and good sparkle; brilliant. A thick, leggy wine with heavy color extraction. Nice, distinguished nose; good fruit but closed up a bit. Very fruity smells; passion fruit or possibly pineapple in a nice medium-sized bouquet with a trace of mint. Light, sprightly; some wood showing behind a cedar aroma. Not particularly complex; still seemingly youngish; developing nicely.

Nice, well-made wine; attractive berry-like fruit; good body and balance. Lots of black cherry Cabernet fruit with wood overtones; tannin level is good. Medium bodied best describes it; not as much fruit in the mouth as there is in the nose. Youth in nose carries to flavor: dry, fruity; excellent first hit. Youthful, astringent with nice fruity full flavor developing; green stemminess with a tart finish.

Some berry-like qualities and good flavors tailing off into a nice moderate finish; tannic at the end; not very exciting. Aftertaste is pretty long and astringent at the moment; this is a restrained Cabernet though near maturity. Sharp and acidic; bottle age may help but will probably retain the acidity. Fascinating, but finally a bit too simple; nevertheless, a hard wine to fault.

Winery produced 1650 cases which were bottled in September 1980 and released in April 1981. Composition is 100% Cabernet with a regional appellation of the Carmel Valley in Monterey. The wine is a current release and is available both in distribution and at the winery.

Dutcher Creek   **1978**   **Unfiltered**   **$4.99**   **F**

Score group F: Poor   Composite score 8.3

Light purple with ruby highlights; clear with medium legs.
Light, rather Gamay style nose with a vinous aroma. A bit peculiar
overall, with an oily, light smell reminiscent of Parmesan cheese.
Light body with a thin, herbal flavor. Tastes like sourdough bread, or a bit
like a nouveaux wine, but without much fruitiness.
Moderate finish with a light, rather sweet aftertaste. Overall, a wispy and
basically unattractive wine.

Winery produced less than 2500 cases. Composition is 97.7% Cabernet
and 2.3% Merlot with a Sonoma and Alexander Valley regional
appellation. This data was taken from the label; winery data not available.

Edmeades Vineyards   **1977 $6.50   D**

Score group D: Good   Composite score 11.6

Medium purple; very clear with medium legs.
Modest nose showing some raspberry fruitiness; has a rough, rather
rubbery overtone that is both disconcerting and unpleasant.
Light body; rather crisp and austere. Some light fruit flavors like black
cherries. Nicely balanced with good acid and a touch of wood.
Short finish with the unpleasant, rubbery quality returning in the
aftertaste. No charm, but no nonsense.

Winery produced 1000 cases which were bottled in September 1979 and
released in April 1980. Composition is 85% Cabernet and 15% Merlot
with a Mendocino regional appellation. This is not the current release
but is still available in distribution. The current releases are 1978
Cabernet (Estate) and 1978 Cabernet (Carney Vineyard) which were
released in April 1981.

Estrella River Winery   **N / V   San Luis Obispo $4.99   C**

Score group C: Very Good   Composite score 11.9

Deep purple with bluish highlights; very clear with moderate legs.
Very young nose with nice fruit; a minty and vegetable aroma with
a stemmy overtone. Very fresh, young berry quality.
Medium body with some nice flavors; nice young fruitiness. Some acid
but overall soft and no complexity.
Moderate finish with a pleasant aftertaste. Overall, a very young, very
simple wine; not unpleasant, but not to be taken seriously.

Winery produced 5000 cases which were bottled in Fall 1980 and
released in the Spring of 1981. Composition is 100% Cabernet with
a San Luis Obispo regional appellation. The wine is currently available
both in distribution and at the winery. This is a second label and is not
considered by the winery as their current release. The current release is
the 1977 Cabernet listed below.

Estrella River Winery   **1977**   **Estate Bottled**   **$8.99**   **C**

Score group C: Very Good   Composite score 11.9

Medium to deep purple with ruby highlights; very clear with medium
to heavy legs.
Moderate nose with some light fruit; harsh, rather weedy aroma in
the background.
Medium body; nicely tannic with some fruit and light but good Cabernet
flavor.
Medium finish with a woody aftertaste. A firm, rather austere wine with
no significant defects.

Winery produced 7500 cases which were bottled in Spring 1979 and
released in the Fall of 1979. Composition is 100% Cabernet; the wine is
estate bottled with a San Luis Obispo regional appellation. The wine is
a current release and is available in limited quantities both in
distribution and at the winery. The next release is scheduled for
Summer to Fall 1981.

Felton Empire   **N / V**   **Maritime Series**   **$4.75**   **F**

Score group F: Poor   Composite score 7.8

Very light ruby with a touch of purple in the highlights; very clear, so
clear that it looks as if it had been filtered several times; thin legs.
Classic "bell pepper" aroma with a touch of spice. Nose has a strange
ashy or chemical overtone, unpleasantly reminiscent of a hospital room.
Light and soft, with no bite or substance; tastes like shellac smells.
Strange, slightly sweet quality, unfortunately not from fruit but rather like
the taste of chemical sweeteners.
Overall, a wine that gives the impression of having been more
manufactured than vintified.

Winery produced 2000 cases which were released in February 1980.
Composition is 65% Cabernet, 23% Merlot and 12% Zinfandel. No
regional appellation is given, but the winery informs us that the grapes
came from Santa Cruz, San Luis Obispo and Santa Barbara counties and
were a combination of the 1978 and 1979 vintages. The wine is
currently available both in distribution and at the winery. The next
release will be in September 1981.

Felton Empire   **1978**   **Hallcrest-Beauregard**   **$12.49**   **D**

Score group D: Good   Composite score 11.1

Medium to full purple; very clear with heavy legs.
Rich, rather perfumey aroma, with some barnyard overtones. Pleasantly
woody behind the perfume.
Medium body with excessive, overpowering tannin. Some nice fruit with
attractive, violet-like flavors but they are masked by the tannic bitterness.
Long, rather flat finish, with some fruit finally showing at the end. A big,
plummy wine in a raw, early state. Impossible to guess where it will
finally end up.

Winery produced 200 cases which were bottled in November 1980 and released in Spring 1981. Composition is 100% Cabernet with a Santa Cruz regional appellation from the named vineyards. The wine is a current release and is available in distribution but not at the winery. The next release is scheduled for January 1982.

Fenestra   1978 $7.50   B

Score group B: Excellent   Composite score 13.3

Deep, full purple; brilliant with heavy legs.
Nice, rich nose with a definite Cabernet aroma; very clean with a touch of mint.
Medium body; fruity but a bit dull, perhaps a bit low in acid. Lots of fruit, with an attractive spearmint flavor. In balance, but seems precariously balanced, not solidly based.
Clean, long finish with some complexity; some fruit in the aftertaste.
A pleasant, fruity, insinuating wine.

Winery produced 183 cases which were bottled in January 1980 and released in September 1980. Composition is 100% Cabernet with a Napa regional appellation. The wine is a current release and is sold out at the winery although some is still available in distribution. The next release is scheduled for October 1981.

Fetzer   1978   Mendocino   Estate Bottled $7.49   C

Score group C: Very Good   Composite score 13.0

Deep purple; brilliant with heavy legs.
Nice, fresh nose; very clean with a pleasant mixed oak and fruit aroma. Not very complex but has an acceptable tea-like varietal aroma with cherry overtones and a bit of woody vanilla behind.
Medium body; good balance and good flavor with a fair, Cabernet quality. Fruit is hanging back, behind the wood and tannin; good acid backbone.
Modest finish with a nice, herbal aftertaste. Simple, without complexity and a bit hollow; since the wine is hanging back, it's hard to tell where this wine will go.

Winery produced 8000 cases which were bottled in May 1980 and released in January 1981. Composition is 100% Cabernet; the wine is estate bottled with a Mendocino regional appellation. The wine is a current release and is available both in distribution and at the winery. Schedule for the next release is not known at this time.

Fetzer   1978   Mendocino $5.00   C

Score group C: Very Good   Composite score 12.8

Medium purple with lighter royal highlights; very clear with medium to heavy legs.
Clean, medium nose; lightly fruity with a raspberry, almost a muscat, quality.
Light to medium body; nice, fruity flavor. Clean, well balanced and supple. Good acid; tannin comes on strong to mask some of the fruit.
Moderate finish; raspberry aftertaste. Nice, clean, respectable Cabernet.

Winery produced 4500 cases which were bottled in June 1980 and released in January 1981. Composition is 100% Cabernet with a Mendocino regional appellation. The wine is a current release and is available both in distribution and at the winery. Schedule for the next release is not known at this time.

Fetzer   **1979**   **Lake County**   **$4.50**   **C**

Score group C: Very Good   Composite score 12.7

Deep purple; very clear with heavy legs.
Nice, distinguished, vaguely lemony nose with a herbaceous aroma. Not a lot of varietal quality.
Medium body; seems thin with a touch of bitterness. Rather seedy or overly pressed flavor with hints of green olives. Ample tannin.
Short but clean finish with some nice green olives in the aftertaste.
Undistinguished but still quite acceptable.

Winery produced 20,000 cases which were bottled in February 1981 and released in April 1981. Composition is 90% Cabernet and 10% Merlot, both from Lake County. The wine is a current release and is available both in distribution and at the winery. Schedule for the next release is not known at this time.

Field Stone   **1977**   **$9.00**   **A**

Score group A: Excellent   Composite score 15.40

Beautiful rich dark hue; very deep substantial garnet color with beautiful blue tones. Looks like a big wine. Good clarity but not brilliant; heavy legs. Currant nose—some violets, some berries, and some fruit, variously described as very ripe apricots or peaches; also hints of coconut and of bourbon. A big black pool of Cabernet with beautiful wood and fruit in a very open nose with a harmony of young oak and varietal bouquet; very inviting. Has a complex, deep bouquet with a soft subdued mood and a strong, rich Cabernet character; definitely a varietal character but still a bit rough.
Nicely balanced with good acid and extremely strong fruit; medium-rich body with lots of tannin; good, full, rich. The flavors follow the nose, developing a full, fairly fruity California Cabernet flavor. Very tight and understated; good acid but rough with a certain earthiness to its taste. Nice wine but masked by oak all the way through; good for bottle aging. Long, plummy finish; big, dark and aromatic with enough fruit. Beautiful wine; subdued, well balanced with a little complexity and no finesse to speak of at present. Primarily a woody aftertaste, but youth highlights this; could be developing some real complexity. A dusty earthiness in aftertaste; very clove, cinnamon subtleness to its flavor. Will have to be handled carefully; a very big wine!

Winery produced 800 cases which were bottled in Summer 1978 and released in Spring 1980. Composition is 100% free-run Cabernet with an Alexander Valley regional appellation. This is not the current release; the current release is the 1978 vintage Cabernet. The schedule for the next release is not known at this time.

Firestone Vineyard   1977 $7.50   D

Score group D: Good   Composite score 10.7

Deep ruby with purple highlights; very clear with medium legs.
Moderate nose reminiscent of pine or herbs, possibly oregano. Faint
varietal aroma in the background.
Soft and clean; very light flavor. Some tannin but overall lacking in acid;
has an unusual grapey flavor with a woody/herbal quality.
Moderate finish; lacking in character and has a rough, woody aftertaste.
Not an appealing wine.

Winery produced 8000 cases which were bottled in June 1979 and
released in June 1980. Composition is 100% Cabernet with the regional
appellation of Santa Ynez Valley. The wine is a current release and is
available both in distribution and at the winery. The next release is
scheduled for sometime in 1982.

Franciscan   1977 $6.49   C

Score group C: Very Good   Composite score 11.8

Deep ruby with purple highlights; very clear with medium legs.
Medium vinous nose, with some anise and green pepper both showing.
A rich, fruity quality, but not much varietal quality.
Light to medium body with good balance and light fruit. Flavor is
unusual and not entirely attractive—sour green apples and cooked
vegetables; some wood and stems.
Medium finish with a stemmy quality and a sharp, chemical aftertaste.
Well made but marred by unpleasant flavor and lacks the distinctive
power and presence of Cabernet.

Winery produced 10,000 cases which were bottled August 1979 and
released in November 1980. Composition is 100% Cabernet with a Napa
regional appellation. The wine is a current release and is available both
in distribution and at the winery. The next release will be the 1978
vintage; no schedule was given for the release.

Freemark Abbey   1976 $9.50   C

Score group C: Very Good   Composite score 12.4

Deep purple; very clear with heavy legs.
Warm, rather spicy nose; some nice green olive aroma behind. Pleasant
but not very fruity.
Moderate body; some fruit but lacking in the mid-range of flavors. Tannic
and in good balance. Astringent and harsh; lacks enough fruit to carry it.
Rough, stemmy aftertaste; moderate finish with tannin lingering on
the palate.

Winery produced 6775 cases which were bottled in May 1979 and
released in September 1980. Composition is 91.9% Cabernet and 8.1%
Merlot with a Napa regional appellation. The wine is a current release
and is available both in distribution and at the winery. The next release
is scheduled for September 1981.

Freemark Abbey   **1977**   **Cabernet Bosche**   **$13.00**   **C**

Score group C: Very Good   Composite score 12.8

Deep purple with a royal fringe; very clear with heavy legs.
Subdued, clean, and somewhat rich nose; shows some fruit and a woody,
processed smell, almost like apple cider.
A bit light bodied with a good woody / spicy Cabernet flavor. Very tannic
with a definite flavor of tart, green apples.
Moderate finish; very tart aftertaste with quite a bit of tannin. A good
wine, slightly out of alignment at the moment but should blend nicely in
one or two years.

**Winery produced 3107 cases which were bottled in May 1980 and
released in April 1981. Composition is 91.5% Cabernet and 8.5% Merlot
with a Napa regional appellation. The wine is a current release and is
available both in distribution and at the winery. The next release is
scheduled for April 1982.**

Grand Cru   **N / V**   **Lot #CS 767**   **Garden Creek**   **$9.00**   **C**

Score group C: Very Good   Composite score 12.6

Medium ruby with royal purple highlights; very clear with heavy legs.
Nose starts small but develops nicely with some air; very young with
good fruit and a faint varietal aroma, backed by hints of walnuts and spice.
Medium to full body with good fruit; curiously spicy quality with hints of
oak. Very sharp with an austere, tannic, licorice-like flavor. No charm and
little varietal quality showing at this point, but may be just too young.
Short finish with spice and herbs in the aftertaste. A young wine, stiff
in the departure and rather heavy-handed at this point but with some
excellent potential.

**Winery produced 1962 cases which were bottled in April 1980 and
released in May 1980. Composition is 100% Cabernet, blended 50%
from the 1976 vintage and 50% from the 1977, with all the wine
coming from the named vineyard. The wine was a current release at the
time of the tasting, and is still available in distribution in limited
quantities. The current release at the time of publication is the 1978
vintage released in May 1981**

Hacienda Wine Cellars   **1977**   **Unfined / Unfiltered**   **$9.00**   **C**

Score group C: Very Good   Composite score 12.9

Deep purple; brilliant with heavy legs.
Mellow, rather small nose with a smoky quality; modest varietal
fruitiness. Not much in the nose, but what is there is good.
Medium body, with a cedar and spice flavor. High tannin and moderate
fruit in good balance. Nice, weedy, decisively Cabernet flavor, but perhaps
a bit dumb and unsophisticated.
Moderate finish, with a redwood and cedar aftertaste. Seems a bit harsh
and assertive at the end.

Winery produced 300 cases which were bottled in June 1980 and released in August 1980. Composition is 100% Cabernet with a Napa regional appellation. The wine is a current release and is available in very limited amounts in distribution. The next release is scheduled for July 1981.

Harbor Winery   1978   Unfined / Unfiltered $9.00   B

Score group B: Superior   Composite score 14.05

Deep garnet or dark ruby but cloudy, heavy legs. A classic color.
Nice spicy / woody varietal aroma. Spare, greenish nose with some fruit; youthful, fruity, austere but appealing. Smoky, smells like roast duck; acetic overtones and wood note. A confusing bouquet; not bad exactly, just not forthcoming.
Light and rather spicy with modest fruit; medium body and has a tannic, dusty character. Good acidity and balance with a creamy fruit quality; possibly some new oak. Cherry-like flavor; fairly dry; tannin very pronounced; fruit somewhat closed in.
Long fruity finish with a very stemmy / herbal aftertaste. Good wine, nice character. Classic California Cabernet flavor with strawberry added; curious but seductive. An enigmatic wine; quite enjoyable but simple. Finishes better than expected—clean and less tart. The wine gives the impression that this winemaker is better than his raw material.

Winery produced 300 cases which were bottled in June 1980 and released in August 1980. Composition is 100% Cabernet with a Napa regional appellation. The wine was the current release at the time of tasting; however, the wine is no longer available in distribution. Limited amounts may be found at retail. The next release is scheduled for July 1981.

Heitz Cellars   1976   Fay Vineyard $20.00   C

Score group C: Very Good   Composite score 12.0

Medium to royal purple; brilliant with moderate to heavy legs.
Rough, rather unusual nose with a rather complex quality compounded of wet gravel, cherries and pinewood. Pleasant but a bit of bitterness showing. Medium body; light fruit with a rough, dry, tannic flavor. A trace of floral perfume and eucalyptus in the back of the mouth, suggestive of the variety. Full, rather earthy aftertaste with lots of tannin in the finish. A good but heavy-handed and rather clumsy wine like an overly affectionate Great Dane.

Winery produced 12,295 bottles (approximately 1024 cases) which were bottled in August 1979 and released in July 1980. Composition is 100% Cabernet with a Napa regional appellation from the named vineyard. Wine was a current release at the time of tasting and a very limited amount is still available at the winery; none remains in distribution. The next release is the 1977 vintage Fay Vineyard Cabernet which will be released in June 1981.

Heitz Cellars   N / V $6.95   D

Score group D: Good   Composite score 11.1

Medium purple with ruby highlights; very clear with thin to medium legs.
Decent bouquet with some berry-like fruit, but has a woody, rather sour
quality with a touch of cooked fruit behind.
Medium body with good balance. Tastes clean and nicely fruity and
young, with moderate tannin.
Woody aftertaste with a vaguely fruity quality suggestive of Merlot. An
average but admirable Cabernet, with a touch of eucalyptus in the flavor
but not very substantial.

**Winery produced 3000 cases which were bottled in December 1978 and
released in Spring 1979. Winery does not wish to provide exact
composition data, but the majority is Cabernet. The wine is a current
release and is available both in distribution and at the winery. There is
no further release planned at this time.**

HMR   1978 $7.50   C

Score group C: Very Good   Composite score 12.4

Deep purple; very clear with heavy legs.
Nice nose, combining fruitiness and stemminess in attractive
proportions; some unpleasant overtones, slightly dank or moldy.
Medium body with good fruit and an attractive bite. Fair tannin and good
balance. Tastes a bit green and unripe.
Clean, rather long finish with a berry-like fruitiness in the aftertaste.
A sturdy, rather than fat, wine with the beginnings of complexity,
suggesting that some age will enhance its qualities.

**Winery produced 2000 cases which were bottled in July 1980 and
released in February 1981. Composition is 100% Cabernet with a
Central Coast Counties regional appellation. The wine is a current
release and is available both in distribution and at the winery. A further
release of the 1977 Estate Cabernet is planned for June 1981.**

Husch Vineyards   1977 $8.99   D

Score group D: Good   Composite score 10.9

Medium garnet purple with brilliant royal highlights; very clear with
medium legs.
Round, full, rather cheesy nose; not much fruit and a bit of a weedy,
sulphurous quality.
Light and a bit thin on the palate. A medicinal cherry flavor gives a
simple fruitiness that is pleasant but dull.
Finishes short and light, with some fruit and a hint of mustiness in
the aftertaste.

**Winery produced 650 cases which were bottled in September 1978
and released in June 1979. Composition is 100% Cabernet with a
Mendocino regional appellation. This is not the current release and is
no longer generally available. The current release is the 1978 vintage.**

Inglenook   **1976**   **Limited Cask / Cask 48**   **$10.49**   **D**

Score group D: Good   Composite score 11.5

Medium purple; very clear with thin to medium legs.
Light and rather closed nose, with some fruit showing after a few minutes.
Youngish, rather vegetal aroma with a clean, stemmy character.
Medium body; soft with some tannin. Dull, rather acidic and not very
substantial. Light fruit with lots of stems and a touch of cooked beets in
the flavor.
Short finish with a tannic and stemmy aftertaste. This wine seems dull
and overproduced; pleasant enough, and certainly clean and well made,
but lacks richness, style and character.

Winery produced 4500 cases which were bottled early in 1980 and
released in Fall 1980. Winery does not wish to provide composition
data; the wine is estate bottled with a Napa regional appellation. The
wine is a current release and is available both in distribution and at the
winery. The next release is scheduled for Fall 1981.

Inglenook   **1977**   **Estate Bottled**   **$7.49**   **D**

Score group D: Good   Composite score 11.2

Medium purple with a touch of ruby; very clear with medium legs.
Light, clean and rather closed nose with hints of earthiness and flowers.
Medium body, good balance with some nice wood and tannin. Not much
grape flavor and lacks varietal character.
Moderate finish with a slight metallic aftertaste. A good, ordinary, honest
wine—well made and pleasant but not identifiably Cabernet.

Winery produced 24,000 cases which were bottled between late 1979
and late 1980 with release scheduled for approximately six months
after bottling. Winery does not wish to provide composition data; the
wine is estate bottled and has a Napa regional appellation. The wine is
a current release and is available both in distribution and at the winery.
The next release is scheduled for August 1981.

Jekel Vineyard   **1977**   **$8.75**   **B**

Score group B: Superior   Composite score 15.27

Medium purple with ruby highlights; slight amber on edge. Not the
deepest color and some evidence of tartrates; very clear with nice
viscosity and strong legs.
Very slight bell pepper aroma, actually much more like tea; only mildly
varietal but pleasant. Rich; full; herbaceous; possibly central coast.
Fragrant; strawberries in nose. Minty, clean wood and fruit with a ripe
clear eucalyptus character; good vanillin forward in a basically young aroma.
Medium body with some good varietal fruit; has a rich roughness in the
flavor with a full, vaguely herbaceous background. Nice acid backbone
and lots of Cabernet character in the mouth but the wood character
predominates. Big, very tannic, good acidity, slightly weedy; soft, and
fairly forward. Austere and a bit oaky now; could have a little more fruit.
Shows promise; has a good finish and good aging potential. The only

criticism—a touch austere; a little more fruit in the mouth would make this super. Hard, young complexity covered by the tannin and oak. Lots of fruit for a wine so very young and finishes well. Needs time for complexity and depth, and possibly underscored on that account; an excellent wine. A classic Cabernet with woodsy notes.

Winery produced 2200 cases which were bottled in May 1980 and released in December 1980. Composition is 100% Cabernet with a Monterey regional appellation. The wine is a current release and is available both in distribution and at the winery. The next release is scheduled for January 1982.

Johnson's   1976 $8.40   E

Score group E: Fair   Composite score 9.7

Medium purple with ruby highlights; clear with thin legs.
Rough, dirty, sulphurous nose; smells like rotten eggs. Some of the sulphur dissipates after a few minutes, leaving a hot, faintly vinous aroma.
Tastes better than it smells; thin body with some fruit and in balance. Not varietal and some sulphurous bitterness remains in the taste.
Moderate finish; would be a pleasant enough red wine except for the stench.

Winery produced 756 cases which were bottled in September 1978 and released in the Fall of 1979. Composition is 100% Cabernet; the wine is estate bottled with an Alexander Valley regional appellation. This is not the current release and is no longer available in distribution. The current release is the 1978 Cabernet; no 1977 Cabernet was produced.

Jordan   1976 $13.99   D

Score group D: Good   Composite score 10.8

Medium to full ruby with a light purple in the highlights; very clear with thin legs.
Pleasant, medium-sized bouquet with a suggestion of cinnamon toast; not very fruity, but has a marked, vegetal overtone.
Medium body with some black cherry Cabernet flavors. Generally light, soft and very accessible with a touch of oak flavor.
Thin finish with stemmy aftertaste showing some tannin. Overall, a clean clear wine with a light but definite Cabernet quality that calls for immediate drinking.

Winery produced 20,000 cases which were bottled in Summer 1978 and released in Spring 1980. Composition is 87% Cabernet and 13% Merlot with an Alexander Valley regional appellation. This wine was the current release at the time of the tasting, and is still available at retail in major wine shops in limited quantities. The current release as of publication is the 1977 Cabernet which is scheduled for release in May 1981.

Keenan   1978 $12.00   A

Score group A: Excellent   Composite score 15.86

Beautiful, blackberry or deep plum color; you can't see through it. Lots of

color with a heavy, young look; very clear with outrageously heavy legs. The legs are purple and last forever. This wine looks big!
Full, rich, fruity with raspberry and wood and overtones of old violets. Thick, viscous with deep fruit and alcohol and a eucalyptus-mint quality; complex, big and very assertive; leaps out of the glass. Black currant smells hint at some (light) varietal character—cherries, cassis. Shows great promise; smells brawny and alcoholic and has a very masculine and earthy quality; possibly just young but may be the way it's made. Substantial body: thick, tannic and good acid; fair fruit, maybe not enough for the potential. Strong monster wine; very chewy. Very good fruit with tastes of oak. Meaty, rich, big, hard; lots of fruit and everything else. A very big wine with some development but room for considerably more. Very tannic; a veritable pitched battle is going on; too soon to drink but good stuff. Rich, heavy berry-like fruit with the varietal holding back; if it develops the wine will rate much higher. Excellent, except that the wood is overdone in the taste; would like to taste in five years. Long, long finish and plenty going on; some complexity and Cabernet character. Not very amiable at present; a big, thick wine which is impenetrable at the moment; dark, big, but, damn, where is it? This wine will age gracefully over a long period; it is now almost wild—undeveloped, closed-in, too tannic, too heavy, too much fruit, i.e. a precisely balanced wine. This is a great wine with lots of "magic."

Winery produced 2000 cases which were bottled in June 1980 and released in October 1980. Composition is 100% Cabernet with a Napa regional appellation. The wine is a current release but is sold out in distribution; however, a limited amount is available at the winery for retail sales. The next release will be the 1979 vintage and is scheduled for October 1981.

Kenwood   1978 $8.50   C

Score group C: Very Good   Composite score 12.0

Deep purple; very clear with heavy legs.
Subdued, rather reluctant nose; herbal and leafy with a bit of the black cherry varietal aroma. Some vaguely unpleasant overtones, described variously as smelling like burnt toast or old sweat socks.
Moderate body; some good fruit with a nice flavor blended of herbs and black cherries. Some tannin and lots of wood.
Long finish with a woody aftertaste and an oxidized impression on the palate—like a touch of raisins. Sound wine of good character, but an overall impression of being too light and watery.

Winery produced 2000 cases which were bottled in May 1980 and released in September 1980. Composition is 63% Cabernet and 37% Merlot with a Sonoma Valley regional appellation. The wine is a current release and is available both in distribution and at the winery. The next release is scheduled for February 1982.

Kenwood   1978   Jack London Vineyard $10.00   C

Score group C: Very Good   Composite score 11.9

Deep purple; very clear with heavy legs.

Full but subdued nose with an overtone of redwood; a bit of fruit and
some decent varietal aroma.
Medium to full body with some nice fruit and a fair amount of tannin.
Very stemmy flavor with acid, fruit and wood well balanced.
Nice aftertaste but surprisingly quick finish. A good and drinkable
mouthful of wine but lacks zest and varietal character.

Winery produced 1000 cases which were bottled in May 1980 and
released in September 1980. Composition is 100% Cabernet with a
Sonoma regional appellation from the named vineyard. The wine is
a current release and is available both in distribution and at the winery.
The next release is scheduled for September 1981.

Charles Krug 1977 $5.99 D

Score group D: Good Composite score 11.6

Royal purple but rather light in hue; very clear with medium legs.
Nice vinous aroma with a minimum of fruit; some pleasant complexity
hints at depth, with overtones of green olives and a rough, chemical
quality behind.
Medium body; some nice fruit flavors and some tannin in balance. Light
overall in the mouth and soft; lacks varietal flavor.
Moderate finish with an unattractive, metallic aftertaste.

Wine is in continuous production. Composition is 100% Cabernet from
the Napa Valley. The wine is a current release and is available both in
distribution and at the winery. This will be the current release
throughout 1981.

Lambert Bridge 1978 $8.29 C

Score group C: Very Good Composite score 11.7

Medium ruby; very clear with thin to medium legs.
Soft, rather lemony nose with light fruit behind. Innocuous, with only a
hint of varietal character.
Thin body; tannic and lightly fruity.
Short finish with a bitter aftertaste like some herbal teas. Very ordinary.

Winery produced 3000 cases which were released in January 1981.
Composition is more than 90% Cabernet and less than 10% Merlot with
a Sonoma regional appellation. This is the current release but is sold
out at the winery and only available in limited quantities at retail. The
next release will be the 1979 vintage to be available in January 1982.

Lawrence Winery 1979 $7.99 D

Score group D: Good Composite score 11.6

Medium to full purple; very clear with medium legs.
Full, rather fruity nose with overtones of spices—woodruff and allspice.
Very young, with a candied quality like blackberry soda pop.
Light body; slightly sweet, fruity flavor and a bit of spritz. Lively, acidic
and tannic with fruit predominating; attractive but not varietal.
Light finish with an unusual bitter, chemical aftertaste. Odd character
and a bit coarse.

Winery produced 2500 cases which were bottled in December 1979 and released in January 1980. Composition is 100% Cabernet with a California appellation. The wine is a current release and is available both in distribution and at the winery. The next release is scheduled for 1984.

Le Fleuron   1978 $6.75   B

Score group B: Superior   Composite score 14.41

Nice plum color with a little depth; a good color—full, clear, good extraction but thin appearance. Clear with medium to heavy legs. Medium fruity bouquet in a pleasant opening salvo. Woody, earthy; some substance with grape overtones and a (not overwhelming) hint of Cabernet. Has a chocolatey fullness with a herbaceous, somewhat bell pepper, character. Decent fruit, clean bouquet, but very undeveloped. Good, medium-rich body, nicely balanced. Has a herbaceous character in the mouth; lots of green olives. Maintains a beautiful texture and flavor—harsh and heavy at once, like an unsweetened honey. Well put together with good fruit and good acid but minimal Cabernet character. Pretty pleasant with perhaps a hint of sweetness. Very berry, like cranberries; well-structured, relatively assertive wine with good fruit and a bit of spice. A little short on finish but nice complexity, with a stemmy, slightly bitter aftertaste. An older style Cabernet, slightly harsh but lively; will benefit from a bit of age. Clear Cabernet Sauvignon character but a trifle dry and woody for comfort.

Winery produced 2300 cases which were bottled in June 1980 and released in September 1980. Composition is 92% Cabernet and 8% Merlot with a Napa regional appellation. This is an alternative label of Joseph Phelps. The wine is a current release and is available both in distribution and at the winery. The schedule for the next release is not available.

Liberty School   1976   Lot 6 $4.99   D

Score group D: Good   Composite score 11.3

Medium purple with a touch of orange in the fringes; clear with medium legs.
Light nose with an undistinguished, vinous aroma.
Light body; very soft and supple. Good vinous character with a trace of tannin.
Short finish with a bitter, tobacco-like aftertaste. Overall, undistinguished and indistinguishable.

Winery produced 12,000 cases which were bottled in January 1980 and released in February 1980. Composition is 100% Cabernet with a Napa regional appellation. This is an alternative label of Caymus. The wine is a current release and is available both in distribution and at the winery. The next release will be Lot 7 and is scheduled for October 1981.

Llords & Elwood   N / V   Cuvee 9 $5.99   D

Score group D: Good   Composite score 10.8

Light to medium ruby; very clear with medium legs.
Youngish, rather fruity nose with a bit of varietal aroma; undistinguished

but not unpleasant.
Medium body with some tannin. Light and lively on the palate with some spritz evident; some fruit but essentially simple.
Short finish with tannic aftertaste. Clean and clear-cut Cabernet but too light and no charm.

Winery produced 1671 cases which were bottled in July 1979 and released in Fall 1979. Composition is 98% Cabernet. The wine is a current release and is available in distribution. The next release is scheduled for Fall 1981.

Louis Martini   1977 $4.99   E

Score group E: Fair   Composite score 9.0

Medium ruby with a touch of purple; clear with medium legs.
Moderate vinous aroma; rather bland and uninviting with overtones of moldy wood and glycol or some chemical.
Light body with a rather sharp and bitter quality, and a bit of green pepper flavor.
Short finish with a sharp aftertaste. A dull, run-of-the-mill, harmless sort of wine, but not Cabernet.

Winery produced 130,000 cases which were bottled early in 1980 and released in Summer 1980. Composition is 90% Cabernet and 10% Merlot with a California appellation. The wine is a current release and is available both in distribution and at the winery. The next release will be the 1978 vintage and is scheduled for August 1981.

Maddalena Vineyard   1977 $6.95   C

Score group C: Very Good   Composite score 11.9

Medium ruby; very clear with medium legs.
Light nose with some moderate varietal aroma. An overtone of weeds or perhaps wet cardboard.
Medium body; light fruit but not much flavor or interest. Moderate tannin and a nice, round quality in the mouth without any corresponding complexity.
Moderate finish. A pleasant, drinkable and uninspired Cabernet.

Winery produced 560 cases which were bottled in October 1979 and released in December 1979. Composition is 100% Cabernet with a Sonoma regional appellation. This is an alternative label for San Antonio Winery. The wine is the current release and is currently available in limited amounts at the San Antonio retail outlets. The next release is the 1978 vintage scheduled for June 1981.

Paul Masson   N/V $5.80   E

Score group E: Fair   Composite score 10.1

Light ruby; very clear with thin legs.
Light nose with a touch of fruit; vinous, not varietal.
Light, thin and tannic; acidic but light in fruit leaving a harsh impression.
Light finish with a slightly cloying aftertaste of wood and walnuts.

A clean, basically acceptable wine but too attenuated in flavor to go far.

Winery produced 75,000 cases which were bottled in August 1980 and released February 1981. Composition is 61% Cabernet, and 39% Merlot, Zinfandel and other mixed red grapes. The wine is a current release and is available both in distribution and at the winery.

Mayacamas   1976   California $16.00   C

Score group C: Very Good   Composite score 12.3

Royal purple with a high extract level that coats the glass; very clear with moderate to heavy legs.
Clean nose, a bit closed and unfriendly. Some light fruit; no Cabernet quality stands out, but one senses a certain richness.
Medium body; astringent, almost chalky, with light fruit and substantial tannin. Flavor obscured but not unpleasant.
Medium finish with an extremely tannic aftertaste. A well-made wine, made in a very "big" style, hence very tannic and rather clumsy; might mellow out in time.

Winery produced 1300 cases which were bottled in July 1979 and released in October 1980. Composition is 90% Cabernet and 10% Merlot with a California appellation. The wine is a current release but is no longer available in distribution; however, a limited amount may still be available at retail. The next release will be the 1977 vintage and is scheduled for release in October 1981.

Mc Lester   N/V $7.50   D

Score group D: Good   Composite score 11.5

Light royal purple with blue highlights; a dark, rich look almost like a bruise. Very clear with heavy legs.
Reluctant nose with a light, fruity and rather minty aroma. Vinous, with a trace of cherries; nothing varietal.
Light body and very fruity; has an almost nouveaux character. Slightly harsh and bitter with a grape juice quality and no varietal flavor.
Finish is hard; very light and fruity aftertaste. This is an interesting but very young wine.

Winery produced 300 cases which were bottled in January 1981 and will be released in July 1981. Composition is 100% Cabernet. The wine is a current release and is available both in limited distribution and at the winery. The wine we received was a pre-release bottle, based on the availability schedule given.

Mc Lester   N/V   Lot J $9.50   C

Score group C: Very Good   Composite score 12.4

Medium purple with blue highlights, looks very young and grapey; very clear with heavy legs.
Clean, light nose showing some fruit but not very varietal. Closed in and definitely in a light style.
Light body; very young flavor. Some fruit and a dusty, black cherry

quality showing some varietal flavors. Very young character and rather weak, without much depth.
Short finish; some nice fruit in the aftertaste with a rather tannic overtone. Good, drinkable wine; very young, perhaps a recent bottling, and in a light style for current drinking.

Winery produced 100 cases which were bottled in January 1981 and will be released in July 1981. Composition is 100% Cabernet. The wine is a current release and is available only at the winery. The wine we tasted was a pre-release bottle, based on the availability schedule given.

| **Milano** | **1977** | **Sanel Valley Vineyards** | **$9.99** | **C** |

Score group C: Very Good   Composite score 12.8

Deep purple; brilliant with heavy legs. Fine, dark color.
Nice, rather restrained but very definite Cabernet nose; excellent fruit and some wood overtones.
Medium body; good fruit and acid in balance. Slightly harsh and tannic with a flavor suggestive of new oak. Deep, but restrained Cabernet flavor.
Moderate to long finish; fruity, varietal aftertaste, with an interesting earthy component. Would go better with some more fruit to match the wood.

Winery produced 250 cases which were bottled in Summer 1979 and released in Spring 1980. Composition is 100% Cabernet with a Hopland, Mendocino regional appellation from the named vineyards. This is not the current release and is no longer available in distribution although it is available at retail. The current release is the 1978 vintage from the same vineyards.

| **Mill Creek** | | **1977** | **$7.49** | **C** |

Score group C: Very Good   Composite score 12.2

Deep ruby with purple highlights; very clear with heavy legs.
Decent grapey nose with some varietal aroma in the background.
Medium body; rather high in acid and correspondingly low in fruit.
Pleasant, light and aromatic, but not much of a mouthful.
Short to moderate finish with a lightly fruity aftertaste.

Winery produced 2950 cases which were bottled in August 1979 and released in September 1980. Composition is 90% Cabernet and 10% Merlot with a Sonoma regional appellation. The wine is a current release and is available both in distribution and at the winery. The next release is scheduled for September 1981.

| **Mirassou** | **1977** | **Harvest Selection** | **$8.99** | **E** |

Score group E: Fair   Composite score 10.2

Deep purple; clear with heavy legs.
Moderate nose with an herbal, stemmy aroma. Some tanky, unpleasant overtones give a curious and complex quality.
Medium body; big, dark and fat with some fruit. Full, rich and a bit soft with a stemmy, almost beefy flavor. The bigness of the wine seems to

obscure any varietal fruit.

Moderate finish with a strange, stemmy aftertaste. In many ways, a well-made wine but the unusual flavor leaves an unpleasant impression. One reviewer commented, "Perhaps this is just some regional characteristic, much favored by locals, but I can't drink this stuff."

Winery produced 5137 cases which were bottled in October 1979 and released in the Fall 1980. Composition is 100% Cabernet with a Monterey regional appellation. The wine is a current release and is available both in distribution and at the winery. The next release is scheduled for Fall 1981.

Mirassou   1977   Unfiltered $6.49   E

Score group E: Fair   Composite score 10.2

Medium purple; clear with medium legs.

Moderate vinous aroma with overtones of herbs and cooked asparagus. Unusual and a bit unpleasant with a strange metallic quality.

Medium body with some fruit and in balance; a strong vegetable taste overpowers anything else.

Short finish and a touch of sweetness in the aftertaste. Overall, an unusual and less than charming wine.

Winery produced 15,000 cases which were bottled in July 1979 and released in Spring 1980. Composition is 100% Cabernet with a Monterey regional appellation. The wine is a current release and is available both in distribution and at the winery. The next release is scheduled for Spring 1981, and therefore is probably available at the time of publication.

Robert Mondavi   1978 $12.00   B

Score group B: Superior   Composite score 14.27

Light depth, light hue; brilliant ruby color with hints of purple in the highlights. Brilliant with medium to thin legs.

Modest nose with a light but definite varietal berry character with nice oak overtones. Minty character; a simplish nose with perfumey fruit and minty wood; not deep or complex but clean and a bit closed in.

Light to medium bodied; dry with well balanced tannins, both grape and new wood; well made and well structured in tannin, fruit, and acid, yet not a big mouthful. Nice and round, with excellent Cabernet flavor; perhaps a little short on acid. Good, rather complicated range of flavors, still partially masked by tannin. Clean to a fault; does not deliver a Cabernet impact.

Moderate cherry and cassis finish with some wood/herb aftertaste.

A sound, nicely made, simple Cabernet—not friendly, but substantial; cleaned up and polished; VERY nice but no thrills. A good, well-balanced wine with some aging potential; but lacks complexity and depth, with the wood overshadowing the fruit.

Winery produced 12,000 cases which were bottled in February 1981 and released in Spring 1981. Composition is 91% Cabernet Sauvignon, 8% Merlot, and 1% Cabernet Franc with a Napa regional appellation.

The wine is a current release and is available both in distribution and at the winery. The next release is scheduled for Spring 1982.

Monterey Peninsula   1976   Monterey Cabernet $4.75   E

Score group E: Fair   Composite score 9.3

Light to medium purple with ruby highlights; very clear with medium legs.
Herbaceous and a bit of a vegetable aroma. Overtones of orange and acetone mix uncomfortably to give an unpleasant nose.
Light body with a herbaceous, rather pungent flavor. Not a particularly attractive character and has some tanky, chemical overtones.
Moderate finish, with an aftertaste like orange bitters.

Winery produced 700 cases which were bottled in March 1978 and released in Spring 1978. Composition is 96% Cabernet, 2% Petite Sirah and 2% Zinfandel with a Monterey regional appellation. This is not the current release; the 1978 Shell Creek listed below is current. However, the wine is still available both in distribution and at the winery.

Monterey Peninsula   1978   Shell Creek Vineyards $9.49   C

Score group C: Very Good   Composite score 11.7

Medium to full purple; very clear with heavy legs.
Substantial but closed up nose. Some berry aroma but some curious overtones of orange peel or floor wax.
Full body; a big, solid wine but closed up and rather woody and harsh. Some Cabernet flavor with a trace of caraway seeds. Clumsy and not well balanced.
Moderate finish with some varietal fruit appearing in the aftertaste.
Powerful but dull; promises but doesn't deliver.

Winery produced 900 cases which were released in January 1981. Composition is 100% Cabernet with a San Luis Obispo regional appellation from the named vineyards. The wine is a current release and is available both in distribution and at the winery. The next release will be the 1979 Cabernet in late 1981.

Mt. Eden   1977   Estate Bottled $24.95   D

Score group D: Good   Composite score 10.3

Deep purple; just barely clear with heavy legs.
Pleasant but anonymous nose with a bit of cedar in it. Some fruit with a chocolate overtone and an initial whiff of sulphur.
Medium to full body with some nice, earthy flavors; very high tannin.
A touch of sweetness, or perhaps very high alcohol, makes the wine seem off balance.
Short finish; the excessive tannin leaves an aftertaste like chewing on peanut shells.

Winery produced 150 cases which were bottled in August 1979 and released in the Fall 1980. Composition is 100% Cabernet; the wine is estate bottled. The wine is a current release but is no longer available in distribution; a limited quantity may still be available at retail and is available at the winery. The next release is scheduled for August 1981.

Mt. Veeder   **1978**   **Bernstein Vineyards**   **$12.75**   **C**

Score group C: Very Good   Composite score 12.4

Deep purple with a royal fringe; very clear with heavy legs.
Light nose, with a slight weedy or vegetal tone; hints of oak and mint.
Pleasant but undistinguished.
Medium body with some nice fruit—raspberry and cherry flavors. Some
richness with a cocoa-like quality, heavy and full in the mouth; good
balance with moderate tannin.
Moderate finish; stemmy aftertaste with a touch of a floral, minty quality.
Pleasant, ordinary wine; good but not distinguished.

Winery produced 3300 cases which were bottled in August 1980 and
released in April 1981. Composition is 89% Cabernet and 11% mixed
reds (Merlot, Malbec, Cabernet Franc, and Petite Verdot) with a Napa
regional appellation from the named vineyards. The wine is a current
release and is available both in distribution and, in case lots, at the
winery. The next release is scheduled for Fall 1981.

Mountainside   **1977**   **$6.00**   **C**

Score group C: Very Good   Composite score 12.4

Medium to deep purple; brilliant with medium legs.
Light, rather subdued nose with overtones of wintergreen and lemon oil.
Fruity aroma, but not much Cabernet quality to it.
Moderate body with a stemmy flavor. Clean, lightly tannic and well
balanced, but short on fruit.
Medium finish; aftertaste is dry and dusty and a bit thin on flavor.
Pleasant wine, without much going on.

Winery produced 564 cases which were bottled in November 1978 and
released in Fall 1979. Composition is 100% Cabernet with a Napa
regional appellation. This is an alternative label for Chateau Chevalier.
This is not the current release and is sold out at the winery and in
distribution. There has been a release of the 1978 Mountainside
Cabernet, which is also in very limited supply. No further release is
scheduled at this time.

Obester   **1977**   **Batto Vineyard**   **$6.99**   **D**

Score group D: Good   Composite score 11.0

Medium purple; very clear with medium legs.
Strange nose with an unusual, rather spicy aroma variously described as
marzipan, cloves with cinnamon, and ginger. Pleasant, but very surprising.
Nice, medium body with definite Cabernet character but continuing
overtones of the same spicy quality as evidenced in the nose. Well
balanced, but a bit rough and tannic.
Moderate finish with lots of tannin in the aftertaste; finish is rather flat
and uninteresting. Overall, drinkable but not enjoyable; an idiosyncratic
Cabernet only a proprietor could love.

Winery produced 250 cases which were released in December 1979 after
at least a year in the bottle. Composition is 100% Cabernet with a

Sonoma regional appellation from the named vineyard. The wine is a current release but is sold out in distribution and at the winery. The next release will be the 1978 vintage scheduled for Fall 1981.

Parducci   1978   North Coast $6.00   C

Score group C: Very Good   Composite score 12.1

Deep purple; very clear with heavy legs.
Stemmy nose with some varietal aroma; has a woody, slightly unpleasant character, like oiled redwood.
Medium body; a bit dry and dusty in the mouth. Some pleasant fruit and a definite varietal flavor. Good balance, but on the tannic side and rather harsh in the mouth.
Moderate finish; a touch of fruit in the aftertaste. Agreeable but nothing special.

Winery produced 18,000 cases which were bottled in January 1981 and released in February 1981. Composition is 100% Cabernet with a North Coast regional appellation. The wine is a current release and is available both in distribution and at the winery. No schedule was given for the next release.

Pedregal   1977 $7.00   C

Score group C: Very Good   Composite score 13.1

Deep purple; very clear with medium to heavy legs.
Nice, soft nose with a kind of bubble-gum fruitiness and oak overtones. Clean, not much varietal character and perhaps a slightly rubbery quality.
Full body; good balance and lots of fruit with a vaguely cherry flavor. Some wood and moderate tannin. Perhaps a bit low in acid, tending towards flabbiness.
Moderate finish; warm, vaguely fruity aftertaste. A nice, soft wine of good character but not varietal enough or distinguished enough.

Winery produced 1000 cases which were bottled in May 1978 and released in November 1978. Composition is 96% Cabernet and 4% Merlot with a Napa regional appellation. This is an alternative label of Stags' Leap Winery. This is not the current release and is no longer available in distribution. The current release is the 1978 vintage under the same label. The next release will be in November 1981.

J Pedroncelli   1978 $5.00   C

Score group C: Very Good   Composite score 12.1

Medium to deep purple; very clear with heavy legs.
Moderate nose with a fruity, herbal aroma. Shows some wood in a rather soft and closed bouquet.
Moderate body and decent balance, but not much substance. Nice herbal or tea-like flavor and some fruit. What flavor is evident is definitely Cabernet. Long finish but flattens out and seems rather dull. Sound wine with no great flaws, but dull and clumsy.

Winery produced 9700 cases which were bottled in January 1981 and released in April 1981. Composition is 100% Cabernet with a Sonoma regional appellation. The wine is a current release and is available both in distribution and at the winery. The next release is scheduled for February 1982.

Pendleton   1978 $9.00   A

Score group A: Excellent   Composite score 15.57

Medium plum color; high extract, looks big. Somewhat murky/cloudy with good legs.
Warm and attractive; a modest, grapey perfume with oak on top and some bouquet. Not much nose, but what there is is clear and crisp with a bit of slightly stalky fruit. Dusty, earthy, good weedy Cabernet fruit and a slightly acetic note. Lovely flowers and oak; memorable.
Nice clean "pruney" fruit with good weedy Cabernet flavors; medium bodied; good acid balance. Feels like there is sand or earth lurking in the background. A nice mouthful of wine; good balance and a nice varietal character with a rich fruitiness. Strong, hard, rich; very meaty. Very French in acidity and aftertaste.
Big and dark; not hard, but restrained; although clear in fruit and flavor; decidedly attractive. Nice, long finish; some complexity—not complicated but fine relationships with what's there. Young, slightly bitter in aftertaste now but should mature out. Good earthy finish; a very California Cabernet.

Winery produced 375 cases which were bottled in August 1980 and released in Winter 1980. Composition is 100% Cabernet from Preston Vineyard in the Napa Valley. The wine is a current release and is available in very limited amounts both in distribution and at the winery. The next release is scheduled for late 1981.

Mario Perelli-Minetti   1977 $5.99   D

Score group D: Good   Composite score 11.3

Medium ruby with a touch of purple; very clear with medium legs.
Friendly nose, well put together but dull and simply vinous.
Good body with good fruit and flavor, but simply grapey, not Cabernet. Low acidity and slightly harsh.
Medium finish. Definitely an average, rather ho-hum red wine.

Winery data not available.

Joseph Phelps   1977 $10.75   B

Score group B: Superior   Composite score 14.75

Beautiful plum color or deep purple; slightly opaque, not brilliant; looks not filtered. Strong legs.
Some reasonable bouquet; a suggestion of sage. Deep, dark cherry overtones; lots of fruit; black currants, flowers; quite nice. Great black cherry/Napa hills nose with high eucalyptus overtones; delightful and unique. Very forward; sappy; a tad green. Oak is predominant and shows more acid and alcohol than bouquet. Beechwood style oak—hot but with strong varietal character pushing through.
An excellent wine: good wood, o.k. acid, maybe just a bit too astringent.

Well balanced and well rounded with a minty taste. Some nice cherry in the fruit and big on tannin, locked-in fruit is masked by oak or tannin. Dusty, full, a trace of eucalyptus. Big, good young wine; quite dry but showing signs of richness.

Drinking well; firm and full with the canonical flavor. Good Cabernet flavors and heaps of fruit. Finish could be longer. Very pleasant; assertive; nice complex of flavors. Not particularly big or complex, but soft and drinkable. Finesse will come in time; when this wine rounds out, it should be super.

Winery produced 6000 cases which were bottled in July 1979 and released in June 1980. Composition is 94% Cabernet and 6% Merlot with a Napa regional appellation. This wine was the current release at the time of the tasting; however, the 1978 vintage is scheduled for June 1981. The 1977 vintage is still available at retail, however.

Joseph Phelps	**1977**	**Backus Vineyards**	**$15.00**	**C**
Score group C: Very Good			Composite score 12.3	

Deep purple with high color extract coating the glass; clear with heavy legs. Rich, rather spicy nose with a nice, unusual quality. Some good varietal aroma, with a honeyed sweetness suggestive of some blended grape. Full body; herb or spice flavor without a lot of fruit or grape character. Very dark and tannic — too much, which obliterates any real fruit. Long to medium finish; a complex aftertaste lost in the wood and tannin. Definitely overly tannic and somewhat retarded but seems to have potential.

Winery produced 530 cases which were bottled in December 1979 and released in March 1981. Composition is 95% Cabernet and 5% Merlot with a Napa regional appellation from the named vineyards. The wine is a current release and is available both in distribution and at the winery. The next release is scheduled for March 1982.

Pine Ridge	**1978**	**Rutherford District**	**$6.95**	**B**
Score group B: Superior			Composite score 15.10	

Medium to dark plum-like color; beautiful shade, clear but not deep; brilliant with heavy legs.

Elegant, spare nose with intimations of good fruit and some breeding. Rich, softly complex with a slight eucalyptus tone — a good Cabernet aroma. Balanced wood; clean and forthcoming, with overtones woven of cocoa, vanilla, and cloves. Lovely, complex, with a marriage of grape and wood.

Moderate body; tannic and a good range of flavors but a bit too much astringency, given the body and fruit. Appealing, somewhat light berry-like fruit, but an undeviating Cabernet flavor. Nicely balanced; well put together. Sharp impact, but smooth on the back of the tongue and magnificent finish. Slightly tannic but bottle age will soften and marry. Nice but short finish with some complexity and an aftertaste like endive. Has slightly rough edges, but good potential. A bit thin on the follow through; nevertheless, a solid wine with some elegance but not much finesse. Good now and potential for more.

Winery produced 4440 cases which were bottled in December 1980 and released in March 1981. Composition is 100% Cabernet with a Napa regional appellation in the Rutherford district. The wine is a current release and is available both in distribution and at the winery.

Rancho Yerba Buena

1976 $5.25   D

Score group D: Good   Composite score 10.6

Medium ruby with purple highlights and a touch of orange; very clear with medium legs.
Not much nose, and what is there has a hot, vaguely raisiny quality. Has a touch of volatile acidity; not attractive.
Thin body and rather acidic; raisiny flavors blended with a taste like shellac. Soft tannin and some moderate fruit but nothing varietal or interesting.
Moderate finish with a woody aftertaste and a bit of tannin. An unusual, rather enigmatic wine.

Winery produced 10,500 cases which were bottled in November 1977 and released in Spring 1978. Composition is 80% Cabernet and 20% Ruby Cabernet with a California appellation. This is not the current release and is not available in distribution any longer although limited amounts may still be available at retail. The current release is the 1978 vintage Cabernet. This is an alternative label for Angelo Papagni Vineyards.

Ravenswood

1977   El Dorado $8.75   D

Score group D: Good   Composite score 10.5

Medium ruby with a touch of orange in the highlights; very clear with medium legs.
Light, simple nose with overtones of strawberries and wood. Rather closed, but some nice fruit behind; aroma more like a Pinot Noir than Cabernet.
Medium body and little fruit; high tannin is out of balance with the remainder of the components. Sharp, light; a minor wine.
Austere finish with a lot of tannin evident; woody aftertaste.

Winery produced 250 cases which were released in the Spring of 1980. Composition is 92% Cabernet and 8% Merlot with an El Dorado regional appellation. This was the most current release of this appellation from the winery at the time of the tasting, although they also have a 1978 Olive Hill Cabernet released more recently. The wine is no longer available in distribution, but the 1978 El Dorado is scheduled for release in July 1981.

Martin Ray

1976 $15.00   F

Score group F: Poor   Composite score 8.3

Deep purple with rich, ruby highlights; clear with heavy legs.
Weedy, rather vegetable aroma—like cooked carrots; has a smoky, stinky nose with a touch of fruit unpleasantly suggestive of moldy apricots.

Medium body; lacks fruit and varietal character. Very dry with moderate tannin but off balance giving a soft harshness on the palate, described by one reviewer as "velvet sandpaper."
Unusual finish with a smoky, rather bitter aftertaste like soy sauce.
Overall, an unusual and bizarre wine that left a complex and disturbing impression.

Winery produced 250 cases which were bottled in March 1980 and released in Fall 1980. Composition is 100% Cabernet with a California appellation and an additional label subtitle of Howell Mountain, Napa. This is not the current release although the wine is still available in limited amounts at the winery. The current release is Cabernet/Merlot Cuvee 778.

Raymond   1978 $9.50   B

Score group B: Superior   Composite score 13.3

Deep purple; very clear with heavy legs.
Pleasant, fragrant nose with a minty, vegetal tone. Some medium varietal aroma; a bit of roughness shows too.
Full body; very nicely balanced with good flavors that echo the mint and vegetable, almost bell pepper, quality in the nose. Soft, nice fruit. Wood, acid, and tannin are all o.k. and well meshed.
Moderate finish; rather on the sweet side. Overall, a pleasant, drinkable, standard Cabernet; its only drawback is the bell pepper quality.

Winery produced 5200 cases which were bottled in August 1980 and released in April 1981. Composition is 80% Cabernet and 20% Merlot with a Napa regional appellation. The wine is a current release and is available both in distribution and at the winery. The next release is the 1979 vintage scheduled for April 1982.

Ridge   1977   York Creek $12.00   C

Score group C: Very Good   Composite score 12.5

Deep purple with rich, warm ruby highlights; brilliant with heavy legs.
Medium nose with a rich quality; definite Cabernet aroma with peppery or green olive overtones.
Full to medium body; very tannic and stemmy but with some nice fruit showing and a definite Cabernet flavor. Good balance and acid but rather rough and overbearing, with a flavor in the back of the mouth like a combination of dried apricots and ginger.
Long finish showing some complexity and finesse; rough aftertaste with a very tannic flavor.

Winery produced 5000 cases which were bottled in September 1979 and released in August 1980. Composition is 96% Cabernet and 4% Merlot with a Napa regional appellation, coming from the named vineyards on Spring Mountain. The wine is not the current release but is still available both in distribution and at the winery. The current release is the 1978 York Creek Cabernet.

Ritchie Creek   1977   **Napa / Spring Mountain**   **$11.50**   **C**

Score group C: Very Good   Composite score 13.0

Medium purple with royal highlights; very clear with heavy legs.
Modest, rather closed nose with a serious, elegant quality. Excellent,
strongly varietal aroma but not very fruity.
Medium body and medium tannin; dry and very stemmy. Rather harsh
and uninviting but still nicely complex. Big and still dumb, but varietal
flavor is emerging and shows promise of attractive flavors.
Moderate finish with a slightly sweet character in the aftertaste.

Winery produced 300 cases which were bottled in July 1979 and
released in February 1981. Composition is that of the vineyard, which is
virtually all Cabernet with some Merlot. The wine is a current release
and is available in distribution but not at the winery. The next release is
the 1978 vintage and is scheduled for Fall 1981.

River Oaks   1977   **$4.49**   **D**

Score group D: Good   Composite score 11.0

Medium purple; very clear with medium legs.
Complicated, but not very attractive bouquet, compounded of spices,
Christmas candy, and apples in cream. Very vinous aroma, but no Cabernet.
Light, thin, and tastes like cherry soda pop; it even has some spritz.
Strange, synthetic candy flavor without any apparent Cabernet quality.
Short, sweet finish.

Winery does not wish to provide production data; wine was bottled in
August 1978 and released in October 1978. Composition is 100%
Cabernet with a Sonoma regional appellation. The wine is a current
release and is available both in distribution and at the winery. The next
release is scheduled for Fall 1981.

Roudon Smith   1978   **San Luis Obispo**   **$6.50**   **C**

Score group C: Very Good   Composite score 12.3

Very deep purple; clear but not brilliant with very heavy legs.
Strongly fruity nose with some green stems or vegetables in the smells.
Has an orange marmalade sweetness mixed with a tea-like, rather
varietal, aroma.
Medium body; lots of fruit but with a rough, vegetal taste. Lots of tannin;
has all of the pieces but doesn't seem integrated.
Moderate, rather rough finish. Pleasant wine that promises well; only
major negative factor is the slightly undesirable aroma, carrying on to
the flavor.

Winery produced 950 cases which were bottled in January 1980 and
released in Spring 1980. Composition is 100% Cabernet with a San Luis
Obispo regional appellation. The wine is a current release, but is no
longer available in distribution. It is available, in limited amounts, at
the winery. The next release is scheduled for Spring 1981.

Roudon Smith   1978   Sonoma $7.99   C

Score group C: Very Good   Composite score 12.9

Deep purple; brilliant with heavy legs.
Distinctly minty, floral nose with a musty, vinous aroma. Smells like green peppercorns, with perhaps some vegetal overtones.
Medium body; some light fruit but lacks strong flavor. Moderate acid and tannin; feels heavy in the mouth as though it is high in alcohol.
Moderate finish with a woody, rather tannic aftertaste. Very pleasant, sound Cabernet in a lighter style; drinkable and agreeable.

Winery produced 600 cases which were bottled in June 1980 and released in Fall 1980. Composition is 100% Cabernet with a Sonoma regional appellation. The wine is a current release but is no longer available in distribution. It is available, in limited amounts, at the winery. The next release is scheduled for Fall 1981.

Rutherford Hill   1977 $9.00   D

Score group D: Good   Composite score 11.6

Deep purple with royal highlights; very clear with heavy legs.
Small nose with a modest vinous aroma and a rubbery overtone, reminiscent of Band-Aids.
Medium body with a rather floral or perfumed flavor. Soft, with a sweet harshness and with the rubbery quality returning in the mouth.
Moderate finish. A wine of no particular distinction and possibly with some underlying flaw causing the rubbery character.

Winery produced 12,000 cases which were bottled in Spring 1980 and released in April 1981. Composition is 85% Cabernet and 15% Merlot, with a Napa regional appellation. The wine is a current release and is available both in distribution and at the winery. The next release is scheduled for late Spring or early Summer 1982.

Rutherford Vintners   1977 $7.50   E

Score group E: Fair   Composite score 9.8

Medium ruby with purple highlights; very clear with medium legs.
Skunky, rather off and unpleasant nose; herbaceous aroma with overtones of eucalyptus.
Thin body, rather tannic and off balance. Light fruit taste like unripe pears. Harsh, bitter and flat.
Short finish with a bitter aftertaste; lackluster.

Winery produced 6500 cases which were bottled in April 1980 and released in October 1980. Composition is 86% Cabernet and 14% Merlot, both from the Napa valley; the wine has a Napa regional appellation. The wine is a current release and is available both in distribution and at the winery. The next release will be the 1978 vintage, and is scheduled for October 1981.

St. Clement   1977 $10.95   B

Score group B: Superior   Composite score 13.2

Deep, rich purple with royal highlights; brilliant with moderate legs.
Undeveloped, closed in nose but clean and rather attractive with a
definite but light varietal aroma.
Moderate body; nice and stemmy taste. Well balanced, woody flavors with
good acid and moderate tannin. Just lacks a little of the fruit to be
completely attractive.
Medium to long finish; clean and sharp aftertaste. Big, perhaps too big
for the amount of fruit; aromatic and concentrated but coarse and not
well-defined enough.

Winery produced 1200 cases which were bottled in June 1979 and
released in September 1979. Composition is 100% Cabernet with a
Napa regional appellation. The wine is currently available both in
distribution and at the winery. The current release, however, is the 1978
vintage. The next release is scheduled for September 1981.

San Antonio Winery   N / V   Cask 520 $4.25   C

Score group C: Very Good   Composite score 11.9

Medium purple with ruby highlights; very clear with medium legs.
Small, rather light nose with some nice fruitiness and a light but definite
Cabernet aroma. Some complexity and perhaps a bit of oxidation.
Medium body and rather light in fruit. Decent balance though perhaps
somewhat soft and lacking in acid; pleasant flavor without much
complexity.
Simple but moderate finish with a clean, spicy aftertaste. A nice wine
although not markedly Cabernet.

Wine is in continuous production. Composition is 100% Cabernet and is
a blend of the 1977 and 1979 Cabernets. This is the current release, but
is only available at the winery-operated retail outlets.

San Martin   1977   Limited Vintage (First Blend) $5.85   D

Score group D: Good   Composite score 11.5

Deep purple with ruby highlights; very clear with heavy legs.
Rough, rather herbaceous nose reminiscent of raw cabbage; smells thick,
almost viscous, and has a definite grape aroma but not with a varietal
quality—more like Petite Sirah than Cabernet.
Medium body; light in fruit and has some funny, beet-like flavors.
Moderately high tannin and a very woody taste; there is a funny flatness
in the mouth perhaps suggestive of grapes from warmer areas, or
overcropping, but in any case giving a wine lacking in verve and oomph.
Moderate finish with a tannic and vegetal aftertaste.

Winery produced 13,600 cases which were bottled in July 1979 and
released in January 1980. Composition is 100% Cabernet, being a
blend of several regions: 57% San Luis Obispo, 30% Santa Barbara, and
13% Santa Clara. The wine is a current release and is available both in
distribution and at the winery. There is also currently available a second

blend, a release of 3200 cases. Composition is 100% Cabernet but with a regional blend of 62% Monterey, 21% Santa Barbara and 17% San Luis Obispo which was released in March 1981. The next release will be the 1978 vintage and is scheduled for mid to late summer 1981.

Sanford & Benedict   1978 $10.00   D

Score group D: Good   Composite score 10.5

Very deep purple; clear with medium legs.
Sweet, rather overripe aroma with an oxidized overtone. The nose is reminiscent of a poor Port or grappa.
Full body with a rich, grapey flavor. High alcohol feel in the mouth, and a hot, harsh undertone. Seems a bit sweet—very much like a late harvest-style wine.
Rough finish with a weedy aftertaste; unusual style and little varietal quality. One reviewer commented, "They must have crushed the leaves with it."

Winery produced 1100 cases which were released in December 1980. Composition is 100% Cabernet from the coastal hills of the Santa Ynez Valley. The wine is a current release and is available in distribution. The wine will be re-released in July 1981.

Santa Ynez Valley   1978 $5.75   D

Score group D: Good   Composite score 10.4

Medium to light purple; clear with medium legs.
Harsh, vegetable aroma with a warm, musty overtone reminiscent of beef broth.
Thin and harsh with an unpleasant, vegetable taste. Sour, sharp and unfriendly.
Short finish with a thin, metallic aftertaste.

Winery produced 400 cases which were bottled in August 1979 and released in June 1980. Composition is 90% Cabernet and 10% Merlot with a California appellation. The wine is a current release and is available in distribution. The next release is scheduled for Fall 1981.

Sebastiani   N / V $6.69   D

Score group D: Good   Composite score 11.1

Medium ruby with a touch of purple; very clear with medium to full legs.
Pleasant, faintly woody nose with a very light varietal aroma. Nose is closed with some slight oxidation.
Light in body with some fruit and definite tannin. Clean but on the flat side.
Moderate finish; clean and well-made with an acidic, rather hot and alcoholic aftertaste. Not unpleasant, but the overall impression is of a weak, thin wine not offering much of anything.

Winery produced 10,000 cases which were bottled in July 1979 and released in July 1980. Composition is 95 to 100% Cabernet and is a blend of the 1976 and 1977 vintages. The wine is a current release and is available both in distribution and at the winery. The next release is scheduled for July 1981.

Sebastiani   **1974**   **Proprietor's Reserve**   **$8.99**   **E**

Score group E: Fair   Composite score 9.5

Light to medium ruby with purple highlights and a touch of orange at the edge; very clear with thin legs.
Green, stemmy nose with little varietal character; light vinous aroma with a touch of fruit behind.
Light and thin in body; not much fruit or flavor. Sharp and acidic with a pleasant woody quality, but no varietal character.
Short, sharp finish with some tannin showing, but nothing else. Clean, sound, unassuming wine but without character.

Winery produced 15,000 cases which were released in September 1980. Composition is 100% Cabernet. The wine is a current release and is available both in distribution and at the winery. The next release will be the 1976 Proprietor's Reserve and is scheduled for September 1981. The 1975 vintage has been bottled, but is being cellared for a few more years.

Shenandoah Vineyards   **1978**   **Deaver Vineyards**   **$8.00**   **C**

Score group C: Very Good   Composite score 13.0

Very deep purple, almost blue-black; clear with heavy legs.
Lots of wood and a bit of a herbaceous character in the nose. Blackberries and currants in a strongly varietal aroma but a touch of a hot, penetrating smell behind, reminiscent of a Magic Marker.
Full body with lots of wood and tannin. VERY tannic; the tannin masks everything else. Very deep, very big; some varietal character coming out but needs time.
Finish is full and so heavy as to be unpleasant. Tannin and fruit have to balance out; needs time to mature and integrate.

Winery produced 400 cases which were bottled in May 1980 and released in June 1980. Composition is 100% Cabernet with an Amador regional appellation. The wine is a current release, but is sold out at the winery and no more is available for distribution. No schedule is available for the next release.

Sherrill Cellars   **1977**   **Shell Creek Vineyards /**   **$10.00**   **C**
                                     Shandon

Score group C: Very Good   Composite score 11.9

Deep and rather rich purple; very clear with heavy legs.
Reluctant, rather subdued nose with a trace of fruit showing and hints of violets. A pleasant varietal character shows up with some air.
Moderate body, nicely put together. Some nice fruit with good acid and balance. Very dry in the mouth with lots of wood and fairly heavy tannin.
Moderate finish with a rough, slightly bitter aftertaste like wet earth.
Rough and a bit astringent at this point, but a decent Cabernet which should age well.

Winery produced 100 cases which were bottled in June 1980 and released in October 1980. Composition is 100% Cabernet from the named vineyards with a California appellation. The wine is a current release, but is sold out at the winery and no more is available for distribution. The next release will be a 1978 Cabernet Wiedeman Vineyards and is scheduled for release in July 1981.

Shown and Sons   1978 $7.99   B

Score group B: Superior   Composite score 14.22

Clear, lighter garnet; bright claret color, but tame looking. Brilliant with heavy legs.
Attractive, light bouquet; suggestions of apples—ample, fresh, good simple fruit and a pleasant grapiness. Some nice fruit in nose—cherries or cherrywood and cedar; a pretty prototypical bouquet for this grape. An almost Gamay character with extremely delicate wood overtones.
Light to medium body; stemmy and lots of tannin with good briary, weedy Cabernet flavors. Some good fruit and a dry quality in the mouth with a hint of vegetable character and a cherrywood taste. Tannin still forward; fairly well balanced with some hint of strawberries; quite pleasant but light. Nicely structured; tannin lingers but so does fruit.
Short finish, but lots of fruit or cherries continues in the finish. A pleasant little wine, of minimal complexity; enjoyable, but not a world beater. A fine delicate Cabernet Sauvignon that makes itself known by the variety rather than fruit or power. Solid burgher-style wine; big, fat, a bit too smug but certainly well made.

Winery has released to date 8831 cases in two lots; the first lot was bottled in August 1980 and released in November 1980, while the second lot was bottled in November 1980 and released in April 1981. We did not determine which lot our bottles came from. Composition is 100% Cabernet with a Napa regional appellation. The wine is a current release and is available both in distribution and at the winery. The next release will be the 1979 vintage and is scheduled for April 1982.

Silver Oak   1976 $11.95   D

Score group D: Good   Composite score 10.3

Light ruby; very clear, almost looks watered down. Thin legs.
Light, thin and closed nose with a vinous aroma. A bit of tar and vegetable behind.
Light body and very thin; soft with just a touch of tannin. Balanced and has a nice flavor, but shows no varietal character at all.
Moderate to short finish; woody aftertaste. Pleasant and drinkable, but not Cabernet.

Winery produced 6500 cases which were bottled in July 1979 and released in February 1981. Composition is 100% Cabernet with an Alexander Valley regional appellation. The wine is a current release but is no longer available for distribution or at the winery. The next release will be the 1977 vintage, and is scheduled for February 1982.

Simi   **1974**   **Reserve Vintage**   **$18.00**   **D**

Score group D: Good   Composite score 11.3

Medium to full purple with a deep ruby fringe and orange highlights; very clear with medium legs.
Vegetal, stinky nose with the smell of boiled eggs. Some smoky or stemmy aroma behind with a hot, dusty quality. Complex but unappealing.
Big, sharp and rather tannic. Nicely balanced with a herbaceous fruitiness carrying through to the taste; wood overpowers the fruit on the palate.
Short finish; a solid wine but marred by the unpleasant nose and the lack of finish.

Winery does not wish to provide production data; the wine was bottled in June 1977 and released in September 1980. Composition is 87% Cabernet and 13% Merlot with an Alexander Valley regional appellation. This is the current release of the Reserve Cabernet, and is available in very limited amounts both in distribution and at the winery. No schedule was given for the next release of the Reserve Cabernet.

Simi   **1977**   **Alexander Valley**   **$7.99**   **C**

Score group C: Very Good   Composite score 12.0

Deep purple with some deep ruby highlights; very clear with heavy legs.
Light, rather green wood nose but with a definite Cabernet aroma.
Medium to light body with good balance. Lively fruit with some light, varietal flavor. Rather acidic, almost citric quality.
Modest finish with some complexity; green wood and fruit in the aftertaste. Rather too stiff but the nice varietal qualities carry the wine.

Winery does not wish to provide production data; the wine was bottled in Fall 1979 and released in September 1980. Composition is 88% Cabernet and 12% Merlot, with an Alexander Valley regional appellation. The wine is a current release and is available both in distribution and at the winery. The next release will be the 1978 vintage, and is scheduled for Fall 1981.

Smothers   **1977**   **$7.25**   **D**

Score group D: Good   Composite score 10.6

Medium ruby with some purple in the highlights; very clear with medium legs.
Rough, rubbery or cheesy aroma with an overtone of cherries or pine. Seems to be all surface and no depth.
Light in body; not much tannin; moderate fruit. Has a harshly fruity quality with a flavor of carmelized strawberries.
Moderate finish with a candy-like, carmelized aftertaste.

Winery produced 200 cases which were bottled and released in Spring 1978. Composition is 100% Cabernet, with a Sonoma regional appellation. There is no current release of Cabernet from the winery. This wine is no longer available in general distribution; a limited amount may still be available at retail. The next release will be the 1979 vintage, and is scheduled for October 1981.

Sonoma Vineyards   **1975**   **Vintage Selection**   **$5.99**   **D**

Score group D: Good   Composite score 10.6

Light purple with ruby highlights and an orange edge; very clear with
thin legs.
Light, subdued nose; closed and with a faintly medicinal quality. Opens
up to a smell of black cherries or apples; still light, but more varietal.
Thin and light without much fruit. Some nice flavors, but a lot of tannin
for such a light wine. Lack of fruit combined with high acid and tannin
put the wine out of balance.
Good, very dry finish. A modest wine that appears to improve noticeably
with air.

Winery produced over 20,000 cases which were bottled in January 1978
and released in the Summer of 1978. Composition is 95% Cabernet and
5% Merlot with a Northern California appellation. The wine is a current
release and is available both in distribution and at the winery.

Sonoma Vineyards   **1977**   **Alexander's Crown**   **$13.40**   **C**

Score group C: Very Good   Composite score 12.6

Deep, rather royal purple; very clear with heavy legs.
Rough, definite nose with a nice, black cherry Cabernet aroma. Hints of
some depth but with some vaguely raisiny smells and a high alcohol quality.
Medium body with substantial tannin. A nice, fruity mouthful but overly
rough and astringent now. Shows a lot of wood in the mouth.
Medium finish; rather tannic in the aftertaste. Would be more pleasant
if it were less hard and more fruity; aging will probably improve and
soften it.

Winery produced 7900 cases which were bottled in April 1980 and
released in Winter 1980. Composition is 100% Cabernet; the wine is
estate bottled with a Sonoma regional appellation. The wine is a current
release and is available both in distribution and at the winery. The next
release will be the 1978 vintage, and is scheduled for Winter 1981.

Souverain   **1976**   **Vintage Selection**   **$11.25**   **D**

Score group D: Good   Composite score 11.2

Medium ruby with some purple; very clear with medium legs.
Nice combination of wood and fruit in the nose; aroma is primarily
vinous, with a stemmy, vegetable smell behind.
Medium body; very dry with moderate tannin and some light fruit. Obvious
wood and stems with a floral quality. Tastes dull and somewhat clumsy.
Moderate finish with a floral aftertaste. Well-made wine that is young,
awkward, and lacks both varietal character and charm.

Winery produced 2081 cases which were bottled in September 1980.
Composition is 100% Cabernet from the counties of Sonoma, Napa, and
Mendocino, giving a North Coast regional appellation. The wine is a
current release and is available both in distribution and at the winery.
There is also a 1977 North Coast Cabernet released (not labeled
"Vintage Selection").

Spring Mountain   1978 $12.00   C

Score group C: Very Good   Composite score 11.8

Deep purple with lighter ruby highlights; very clear with heavy legs.
Big nose with some varietal aroma and heavy fruit hiding behind a rough,
stemmy quality.
Medium body with some fruit but everything overpowered by massive
tannin. Has a fresh, rich impression, but lacks any other flavor except
tannin—or at least any other flavors are impossible to discern.
Long but harsh finish with tannic aftertaste. A dark, dumb wine,
inelegant and monochromatic.

Winery produced 10,500 cases which were bottled in June 1980 and
released in October 1980. Composition is 88.5% Cabernet, 7.5% Merlot
and 4% Cabernet Franc, with a Napa regional appellation. The wine is
a current release and is available both in distribution and at the winery. The
next release will be the 1979 vintage, and is scheduled for October 1981.

Stag's Leap Wine Cellars   1978 $8.99   B

Score group B: Superior   Composite score 15.28

Basic medium purple color with a little depth but no brilliance; young
and dark. Bright, clear; heavy legs.
Grassy, damp woods nose and a rich, nice, varietal aroma. Has good
earth/spice overtones and nice fruit beginning to show in nose. Young;
fairly big with emerging fruit and plenty of oak showing. Cedar and spice;
rather stemmy. A serious, if not slightly masked nose; needs time to open up.
Good, big, solid, serious wine; nicely balanced with a rich Cabernet flavor.
Stately and reasonably full-bodied; soft, supple. Elegant with a nice
flavor; slightly vegetal but good solid fruit and a creamy finish. Bit of
rawness; slightly bitter. Tannin and acid still the overall first impression.
Solid, middle-of-the-road stuff: alcohol, fruit, and acid; very pleasant impact.
Good finish but flattens out; a nice, well-made wine with some
complexity. Not too assertive; a nice middle range Cabernet. Flavor
follows nose with a full, rich, vegetal character that adds dimension; true
to varietal with lots of black raspberry character. A well made wine but
drink soon; this wine is not going to be a long-lived great Cabernet but is
a pleasure to drink now and should drink well for a reasonable period.

Winery data not available.

Sterling Vineyards   1976   Sterling Reserve $25.00   C

Score group C: Very Good   Composite score 11.8

Medium ruby with a touch of purple; very clear with thin legs.
Subdued, rather light nose with a skunky overtone. Some pleasant fruit
and wood with some varietal aroma showing along with a touch of
rhubarb behind it.
Light to medium body; nice flavor but not much fruit and a lot of wood.
Good balance and acid, and has a big, vigorous quality that seems to
come from the wood rather than the grape.
Moderate finish with a harsh, woody aftertaste. This wine has more power
than grace and more weight than character; it might improve with time

and bottle age.

Winery produced 3500 cases which were bottled in August 1978 of which 2200 cases were released in September 1980. Composition is 75% Cabernet and 25% Merlot; the wine is estate bottled, with a Napa regional appellation. The wine is a current release and is available both in distribution and at the winery. The next release is scheduled for August 1981.

Sterling Vineyards	**1977**	**Estate Bottled**	**$10.00**	**C**

Score group C: Very Good   Composite score 11.9

Deep ruby with purple highlights; very clear with medium to heavy legs.
Modest, easy nose with faint hints of cherry and an overtone of oak.
Moderate body with good fruit and balance. Very tannic and has quite
a bit of acid.
Moderate finish; backward and very tannic at the end, but with some fruit
to balance it. A generally middle-of-the-road wine, except for the tannin,
which may smooth out over time.

Winery produced 20,000 cases which were bottled in July 1979 and 12,900 cases were released in January 1981. Composition is 75% Cabernet and 25% Merlot; the wine is estate bottled with a Napa regional appellation. The wine is a current release and is available both in distribution and at the winery. The next release will be the 1978 vintage, and is scheduled for August 1981.

Stone Creek			**1977**	**$4.99**	**D**

Score group D: Good   Composite score 10.5

Medium ruby; very clear with thin legs.
Light and clean nose; honest but without any complexity. Soft and rather
stemmy aroma with a raspberry overtone.
Light body and thin flavor. Soft and a bit sharp in the mouth with
a peculiar parsley-like taste.
Short finish with an aftertaste of cashews. A light, drinkable wine without
any varietal qualities.

Winery data not available. Label indicates a North Coast regional appellation.

Stonegate	**1977**	**Steiner Vineyard**	**$7.50**	**C**

Score group C: Very Good   Composite score 12.9

Deep purple; brilliant with heavy legs.
Interesting, minty, green peppercorn nose without any strongly
distinguishing characteristics. Nose overall is more vinous than varietal,
although some varietal aroma is in the background.
Light body with a bit of a spritzy quality; lively, yet very dry. Good balance
with a full round of the flavor of the old eucalyptus.
Moderate finish. A simple, not overly wooded Cabernet, but hardly
any charm.

Winery produced 1011 cases which were bottled in February 1979 and released in October 1980. Composition is 100% Cabernet with a Sonoma regional appellation from the named vineyard. The wine is not a current release but is available both in distribution and at the winery. The current release is the 1977 Napa Valley Cabernet. The next release is scheduled for March 1982.

Stony Ridge   1975 $5.50   D

Score group D: Good   Composite score 11.2

Medium ruby with purple highlights; very clear with thin legs.
Friendly, young Cabernet nose with an anise/cherry quality. Some wood showing behind the fruit.
Medium bodied and a bit flat in the middle; has a rough, rather vegetal flavor and an unusual acidity. Tastes like canned asparagus or vitamin tablets.
Short and sharp finish with a woody, tannic aftertaste. This wine has some backbone and character, but is otherwise unremarkable.

Winery data not available. Label indicates a North Coast regional appellation.

Sycamore Creek   1978 $9.99   C

Score group C: Very Good   Composite score 13.1

Deep purple; very clear with heavy legs.
Modest bouquet with a woody nose and lots of vanilla/oak character. Some good varietal aroma with hints of high alcohol burning through.
Full body; thick, almost viscous in the mouth with some good varietal character. Also some hints of a rubbery or plastic taste behind the fruit. Above all, and overwhelming all, is a huge dose of tannin.
Long finish; tannin masks all else in the aftertaste. Not an especially friendly or welcoming wine at present, but should improve with some age to balance and mellow the tannic character.

Winery produced approximately 800 cases which were bottled in Fall 1980 and released in 1981. Composition is 100% Cabernet, and came from two vineyards in Uvas Valley and one in San Luis Obispo, giving a Central Coast regional appellation. The wine is not a current release but is available both in distribution and at the winery. The current release is a 1979 Cabernet from San Luis Obispo.

Toyon   1976 $5.69   D

Score group D: Good   Composite score 10.4

Medium ruby with a touch of orange in the highlights; very clear with thin legs.
Soft, rather weak nose with a vegetable aroma; smells like carrots and redwood, not Cabernet.
Thin and very tannic and lacking in charm. Some fruit but excessive wood or stems have added so much tannin that it kills all other qualities.
Medium finish, with a stemmy, tannic aftertaste.

Winery data not available. The wine has a Sonoma regional appellation.

Tulocay   1978 $8.49   B

Score group B: Superior   Composite score 15.01

Clear, deep garnet purple with a ruby hue; nice viscosity. Normal, young, average; clean, very transparent; brilliant with medium legs.
Rich, almost perfumey nose with some pleasant fruit and mild varietal character too. Good fruit in nose: clean, minty, and slightly earthy. Well-developed bouquet but not Cabernet fragrance; a mixture of cinnamon and cranberries; fruity, perfumey, almost cosmetic, but its nicest feature. Potentially good fruit; slow to open up but beautiful balance.
Medium body and light fruit in balance, with a tannic, appley character; a nice balance of fruit and wood; slightly acidic and tannic but agreeable. High fruit opening up; substantial but no elegance or subtlety showing yet. Noticeable fruit of the right sort but Cabernet flavor only medium. Very complex and substantial wine; could pass off as a "great claret." Agreeable, raspberry-like finish; perhaps a bit soft with a woody aftertaste. Finish is short, clean, vibrant; elegant. Not heavy-handed; pleasant now but might move in awkward stages. Slightly thin for this judging but excellent fruit, balance.

Winery produced 299 cases which were bottled in May 1980 and released in November 1980. Composition is 100% Cabernet from a single vineyard in the Napa Valley region. The wine is a current release but is no longer available in distribution; however, it is still available at the winery. The next release will be the 1979 vintage and is scheduled for November 1981.

Veedercrest   1977   Richard Seltzner Vineyard $10.35   D

Score group D: Good   Composite score 11.6

Deep ruby with purple highlights; very clear with medium legs.
Nose is soft, closed and has an unfamiliar, complex quality. Aroma of allspice or cinnamon and some varietal fruit behind.
Moderate body; nice berry fruit taste. Not big but pleasant; perhaps a bit flabby and lacking in acid.
Moderate finish; drinks well now but is a mediocre, ordinary wine without any prospects for improvement.

Winery produced approximately 800 cases which were bottled in January 1979 and released in June 1979. Composition is 100% Cabernet with a regional appellation of Napa county from the named vineyard. This is not the current release; the 1978 vintage Cabernet from this vineyard is on the market. The forthcoming release will be the 1979 vintage scheduled for late 1981.

Ventana Vineyards   1978 $9.50   C

Score group C: Very Good   Composite score 11.8

Deep purple; very clear with heavy legs.
Bright, sharp nose with a stemmy, almost tar-like aroma that jumps out of the glass. Attractive but hardly subtle.
Moderate to full body with good fruit. Some stemmy, slightly green

flavors reminiscent of central coast grapes. Unusually forward and aggressive but flavors don't seem to blend well.
Moderate finish with a dark, hollow quality and a rough, hot aftertaste.

Winery produced 600 cases which were bottled in January 1980 and released in March 1981. Composition is 100% Cabernet with a regional appellation of Monterey county. The wine is a current release and is available both in distribution and at the winery.

Villa Mt. Eden   1978   Estate Bottled $12.00   B

Score group B: Superior   Composite score 14.95

Young but a stunning density; deep, rich, light-plum color; brilliant with heavy legs.
Rich, rather Bordeaux-like nose with a definite varietal aroma; still a bit closed and rather complicated. Subdued, delicate nose developing bouquet. One senses the wine in an in-between stage: the fruity youth is gone but there's no bouquet yet. Resinous; nice fruit and wood.
Good balance; nice flavors of earth, tannin and light fruit but wood and tannin dominate. A solid wine but fruit is still obscured and elements of extraneous almond-like flavor show through. Tannic; black cherry flavors with fruit masked partially by tannin. Several tasters suggested new wood a bit overdone; may age to soften more. Good dryness; nice body; good acidity; nicely balanced. Coming round as solid, creamy, big, dry wine; solid California style with proper balance of fruit and acid. Some richness and good balance but very hard, very young, very dry.
Finishes well but no finesse; all wood and an earthy aftertaste. No outstanding characteristics, but will drink nicely; showing some complexity and signs of elegance. Can't tell much about this one; Rocky IV.

Winery produced 2200 cases which were bottled in August 1980 and released in April 1981. Composition is 100% Cabernet; the wine is estate bottled with a Napa regional appellation. The wine is a current release and is available both in distribution and at the winery. The next release will be the 1978 Reserve and is scheduled for Fall 1981.

Vose Vineyards   1978 $11.98   D

Score group D: Good   Composite score 11.3

Medium to full purple; very clear with medium legs.
Deep, rich nose with a hot, brandy-like quality. Some earth and spice behind, but a strong acetic smell predominates. Presumably some excessive volatile acidity.
Medium body with some subdued fruit and good balance. Marred by very harsh flavor and excessive tannin; flavor is retarded by the tannin.
Moderate finish with a bitter, tannic aftertaste; seems like an attempt at a big, heavy-style Cabernet that took a wrong turn.

Winery produced 600 cases which were bottled in Spring 1980 and released in Winter 1980. Composition is 100% Cabernet with a regional appellation of Napa county. The wine is in current distribution and is available at the winery; the next release is scheduled sometime in 1981.

Wilson Daniels   1977 $9.00   C

Score group C: Very Good   Composite score 12.6

Medium ruby with an orange fringe; very clear with medium legs.
Lemon oil or wintergreen nose, very minty and fruity. Smoky, earthy
aroma masking any varietal quality.
Light in body with a touch of stems; good acid makes the wine seem
bright and alive in the mouth. Nicely balanced with a hint of almonds.
Needs more fruit for full potential
Rough, rather lingering finish with an unpleasantly metallic quality in
the aftertaste. A very good wine that simply lacks any interesting or
exciting qualities.

Winery produced 1500 cases which were bottled in March 1979 and
released in September 1979. Composition is 100% Cabernet from the
Napa Valley. This is a current release but is no longer available at the
winery, although it is still available in distribution. The winery released
their 1978 Cabernet Sauvignon in September 1980.

Zaca Mesa   1977   **American Oak** $7.29   D

Score group D: Good   Composite score 11.6

Medium to deep purple; very clear with heavy legs.
Pleasant, slightly minty nose with some nice wood over a light but
definite Cabernet aroma.
Medium body with some fruit; seems a bit hard and high in acid. Has just
a bit of Cabernet flavor.
Long finish with a rough, woody character and a rough, rich aftertaste
with a flavor like braised celery.

Winery produced 2700 cases which were bottled in February 1979 and
released in September 1980. Composition is 100% Cabernet from the
Mariposa and Chapel vineyards at Zaca Mesa Ranch in the Santa Ynez
Valley. The wine is a current release and generally available; the next
release is the 1978 vintage and is scheduled for early June 1981. This
release was one of three for the 1977 vintage, and is distinguished by
the label designation 'Aged in American Oak.'

ZD   1978 $9.49   D

Score group D: Good   Composite score 11.4

Medium to full purple; very clear with medium to heavy legs.
Nice, rather soft and intricate nose; a good varietal aroma but with
a sweet/tart quality that suggests some oxidation.
Medium to full body; some nice fruit and good flavor. Definitely a big
wine with a heavy, clumsy quality like a gravy. Seems burnt or oxidized.
Moderate finish.

Winery produced 972 cases which were bottled in June 1980 and
released in October 1980. The wine is 79% Cabernet and 21% Merlot
with a regional appellation of San Luis Obispo. The wine is a current
release and is currently available at the winery and in distribution
channels. The winery does not presently plan another release of
Cabernet from this area.

RANKING-VALUE TABLES

The following tables are a *California Wine List* exclusive feature.
These tables are designed to help you select the best scoring wines based on taste/quality and price per 750ml bottle.
Please note, the tables are not a substitute for the individual notes on each wine. Your real value from California Wine List publications comes from use of the alphabetic listing to get a more indepth "feeling" for the wine.
The two star.(★ ★) designation is given to wines which offer an outstanding taste combined with excellent value at time of publication.
The one star (★) designation is provided to highlight excellent dollar value within the upper two statistical categories.
Remember, the computerized nature of our scoring and ranking combined with the broadest review of California wines in print helps you make your choices. An informed selection is your best path to satisfaction.

Score	Winery Name	Label Designation	Year	Price

Score Group A: Excellent

Score	Winery Name	Label Designation	Year	Price
15.86	Keenan		1978	$12.00
15.68	Cassayre-Forni		1978	9.00
15.57	Pendleton		1978	9.00
15.47	Cakebread Cellars		1978	12.00
15.41	Duckhorn Vineyards	Napa	1978	10.50
15.40	Field Stone	Alexander Valley	1977	9.00
15.37	Durney	Carmel Valley	1978	11.95

Score Group B: Superior

Score	Winery Name	Label Designation	Year	Price
15.28	Stag's Leap Wine Cellars		1978	$8.99
15.27	Jekel Vineyard		1977	8.75
15.10	Pine Ridge	Rutherford District	1978	6.95 ★
15.01	Tulocay		1978	8.49
14.95	Villa Mt. Eden	Estate Bottled	1978	12.00
14.86	Cakebread Cellars	JT-L1	1978	12.00
14.75	Joseph Phelps		1977	10.75
14.68	Clos du Val		1978	12.00
14.41	Le Fleuron		1978	6.75 ★
14.27	Robert Mondavi		1978	12.00
14.05	Harbor Winery	Unfined/Unfiltered	1978	9.00
13.82	Shown & Sons		1978	7.99
13.48	Almaden	Monterey	1978	4.00 ★
13.3	Fenestra		1978	7.50
13.3	Raymond		1978	9.50
13.22	Clos du Val	Reserve	1977	20.00
13.2	St. Clement		1977	10.95

Score Group C: Very Good

Score	Winery Name	Label Designation	Year	Price
13.1	Sycamore Creek		1978	$9.99
13.1	Pedregal		1977	7.00

Score	Winery Name	Label Designation	Year	Price
13.0	Shenandoah Vineyards	Deaver Vineyards	1978	$8.00
13.0	J Carey Cellars	Alamo Pintado Vineyards	1978	6.00
13.0	Fetzer	Estate Bottled	1978	7.49
13.0	Ritchie Creek	Spring Mountain	1977	11.50
13.0	Chateau Montelena		1976	10.00
12.9	Roudon-Smith		1978	7.99
12.9	Hacienda Wine Cellars		1977	9.00
12.9	Stonegate	Steiner Vineyard	1977	7.50
12.8	Dehlinger Winery		1978	8.00
12.8	Milano	Sanel Valley Vineyards	1977	9.99
12.8	Freemark Abbey	Cabernet Bosche	1977	9.50
12.8	Fetzer		1978	3.69
12.8	Chateau Chevalier		1978	12.50
12.7	Fetzer	Lake County	1979	4.50
12.7	Chateau St. Jean	Jack London Vineyard	1977	9.50
12.6	Sonoma Vineyards	Alexander's Crown	1977	13.40
12.6	Wilson Daniels		1977	9.00
12.6	Grand Cru	Lot #CS 767	N/V	9.00
12.5	Mc Lester	Lot J	N/V	9.50
12.5	Ridge	York Creek	1977	12.00
12.4	Mt. Veeder	Bernstein Vineyards	1978	10.59
12.4	HMR		1978	7.50
12.4	Mountainside		1977	6.00
12.4	Beaulieu Vineyard	Private Reserve	1975	15.00
12.4	Freemark Abbey		1976	9.50
12.3	Burgess		1978	9.00
12.3	Joseph Phelps	Backus Vineyard	1977	15.00
12.3	Carneros Creek	Turnbull/Fay Vineyards	1978	8.50
12.3	Roudon-Smith	San Luis Obispo	1978	6.50
12.3	Mayacamas		1976	16.00
12.2	Alexander Valley		1978	6.49
12.2	Mill Creek		1977	7.49
12.1	J. Pedroncelli		1978	5.00
12.1	Parducci		1978	6.00
12.1	Davis Bynum		1978	7.75
12.0	Chateau St. Jean	Glen Ellen Vineyards	1977	13.50
12.0	Kenwood		1978	8.50
12.0	Diamond Creek	Red Rock Terrace	1978	12.00
12.0	Simi		1977	7.99
12.0	Heitz Cellars	Fay Vineyard	1976	20.00
11.9	Sterling Vineyards		1977	10.00
11.9	Chappellet		1977	11.95
11.9	Beaulieu Vineyard		1977	7.00
11.9	Estrella River Winery		N/V	3.99
11.9	Estrella River Winery	Estate Bottled	1977	8.99
11.9	Kenwood	Jack London Vineyard	1978	10.00
11.9	Sherrill Cellars	Shell Creek Vineyards	1977	10.00
11.9	Maddalena Vineyard		1977	6.95
11.9	San Antonio Winery	Cask 520	N/V	4.25

Score	Winery Name	Label Designation	Year	Price
11.8	Clos du Bois		1978	$7.50
11.8	Ventana Vineyards		1978	9.50
11.8	Spring Mountain		1978	12.00
11.8	Sterling Vineyards	Reserve	1976	25.00
11.8	Franciscan		1977	6.49
11.7	Callaway	Estate Bottled	1978	7.49
11.7	Monterey Peninsula	Shell Creek Vineyards	1978	9.49
11.7	Lambert Bridge		1978	8.29

Score Group D: Good

Score	Winery Name	Label Designation	Year	Price
11.6	Zaca Mesa		1977	$7.29
11.6	Edmeades Vineyards		1977	6.50
11.6	Boeger		1978	7.49
11.6	Lawrence Winery		1979	7.99
11.6	Rutherford Hill		1977	9.00
11.6	Conn Creek		1977	12.00
11.6	Charles Krug		1977	5.99
11.6	Veedercrest	Richard Stelzner Vineyard	1977	10.35
11.5	San Martin	Limited Vintage	1977	5.85
11.5	David Bruce	Santa Cruz	1978	11.95
11.5	Mc Lester		N/V	7.50
11.5	Inglenook	Ltd. Cask/Cask 48	N/V	10.49
11.4	ZD		1978	9.49
11.4	Alatera		1978	10.00
11.4	Cuvaison		1976	9.00
11.3	Vose Vineyards		1978	11.98
11.3	Liberty School	Lot 6	1976	4.99
11.3	Simi	Reserve Vintage	1974	18.00
11.3	Mario Perelli-Minetti		1977	5.99
11.2	Dry Creek Vineyards		1978	7.25
11.2	Souverain	Vintage Selection	1976	11.25
11.2	Stony Ridge		1975	5.50
11.2	Inglenook		1977	7.49
11.1	Heitz Cellars		N/V	6.95
11.1	Felton Empire	Hallcrest-Beauregard	1978	12.49
11.1	Sebastiani		N/V	6.69
11.0	River Oaks		1977	4.49
11.0	Obester		1977	6.99
10.9	Husch Vineyards		1977	8.99
10.9	Cilurzo-Piconi	First Crush	1978	6.50
10.8	Llords & Elwood	Cuvee 9	N/V	5.99
10.8	Clos du Bois	Proprietor's Reserve	1977	15.00
10.8	Jordan		1976	13.99
10.7	Firestone Vineyard		1977	7.50
10.7	Dry Creek Vineyard	Vintner's Selection	1977	10.00
10.6	Rancho Yerba Buena		1976	5.25
10.6	Sonoma Vineyards	Vintage Selection	1975	5.99
10.6	Smothers		1977	7.25

Score	Winery Name	Label Designation	Year	Price
10.5	Ravenswood		1977	$8.75
10.5	Sanford & Benedict		1978	10.00
10.5	Stone Creek		1977	4.49
10.4	Santa Ynez Valley		1978	5.75
10.4	Toyon		1976	5.69
10.3	Silver Oak		1976	11.95
10.3	Mt. Eden	Estate Bottled	1977	24.95
10.3	Beringer		1977	6.49

Score Group E: Fair

Score	Winery Name	Label Designation	Year	Price
10.2	Mirassou	Unfiltered	1977	$6.49
10.2	Mirassou	Harvest Selection	1977	8.99
10.1	Paul Masson		N/V	5.80
9.9	Concannon	Limited Bottling	1973	9.99
9.8	Rutherford Vintners		1977	7.50
9.7	Johnson's		1976	8.40
9.5	Sebastiani	Proprietor's Reserve	1974	8.99
9.3	Cygnet Cellars		1977	5.50
9.3	Louis Martini		1977	4.99
9.3	Monterey Peninsula	Monterey Cabernet	1976	4.75

Score Group F: Poor

Score	Winery Name	Label Designation	Year	Price
8.9	Christian Bros.		1975	$7.35
8.3	Dutcher Creek	Unfiltered	1978	4.99
8.3	Martin Ray		1976	15.00
7.8	Felton Empire	Maritime Series	N/V	4.75
7.2	David Bruce	San Luis Obispo	1977	7.50

ABOUT THE EDITOR: David Holzgang brings a formidable expertise in information handling and extensive wine tasting experience to the California Wine List. His concept for the series (110 Chardonnays, 125 Zinfandels, 161 Jug Wines, and 144 Cabernets) developed when he began to look for accurate, up-to-the-minute information on current releases. Each time he found newsletters reporting on a few available wines, but no publication that compared them all. He set out to provide wine lovers everywhere with a guide that reflects the findings of a broad-based panel of expert tasters. Thus, the California Wine List.

"The massive collection of data is easy to accomplish by computer. Fortunately, it is people and nature that make wine. California Wine List uses computers to report people's feelings about wine," comments David.

The California Wine List panel of tasting experts assembled by David includes two widely read and respected food writers, one locally acknowledged wine merchant, and a major wine maker.